THE MOST AMAZING
FOOTBALL

FACTS FROM THE LAST 150 YEARS

firsts, Lasts & onLys

PAUL DONNELLEY PRESENTS

THE MOST AMAZING FOOTBALL

FACTS FROM THE LAST 150 YEARS

Bounty
Books

DEDICATION

Dedicated, with love, to my parents-in-law, Khaira
and Abdelkader Bendris

An Hachette UK Company
www.hachette.co.uk

First published in Great Britain in 2010 by
Hamlyn, a division of Octopus Publishing Group Ltd

This edition published in 2012 by Bounty Books,
a division of Octopus Publishing Group Ltd
Endeavour House
189 Shaftesbury Avenue
London
WC2H 8JY
www.octopusbooks.co.uk

ISBN: 978 0 753 72328 9

A CIP catalogue record for this book is available from
the British Library

Printed and bound in China

THE FIRSTS

THE FIRST

THE FIRST (cont.)

THE FIRST (cont.)

THE FIRST (cont.)

THE FIRST (cont.)

THE FIRST (cont.)

THE FIRST (cont.)

THE FIRST (cont.)

THE LASTS

THE LAST

THE LAST (cont.)

THE LAST (cont.)

THE ONLYS

THE ONLY

THE ONLY (cont.)

THE ONLY (cont.)

THE ONLY (cont.)

THE ONLY (cont.)

INTRODUCTION

Football is a sport played the world over, and it is also probably the simplest sport in the world to play. A ball can be fashioned from a tin can if a real ball is not available, and who has not played with jumpers or school blazers doubling for goalposts? No kit available? Easy – shirts v skins. Who wins? The team that scores the most goals. It is this very simplicity that has made the sport the world's most popular to watch and to participate in. I know, technically, that apparently more people go fishing each weekend in Britain, but that hardly counts as a sport, more a pastime, and which small boy has ever pretended to his mates that he is Des Taylor?

Football has launched a million fantasies and a million stories. Gathered in this book are several hundred, all categorized as to whether they were a first, a last or an only. In the lasts and onlys categories some of the entries are final and some are last entries to date – for example, it is perfectly possible that a team might win the FA Cup and promotion in the same season. However, the fact that it has only ever been done (by West Bromwich Albion) in 1930–1931 makes it at best highly unlikely. And to judge by the standard of today's politicians, not to mention today's footballers, I think it unlikely that we will ever see another Cabinet Minister who will represent England at football, let alone cricket.

I grew up watching football in the 1970s and collecting sticker albums with stickers that weren't actually sticky and so needed glue to put them into the album. Like many small boys I also collated football facts and figures – who played for whom and who played where. Grounds that I grew up with included Ayresome Park, Filbert Street, Maine Road, Roker Park and, of course, the one that I went to most often, Arsenal Stadium. All of them, with the exception of Arsenal Stadium, fell foul of the Taylor Report, which demanded all-seater stadia for the Premier League and Division One clubs. Arsenal's move was dictated more by financial necessity, being unable to compete with the monetary might of the likes of Manchester United and the top teams they would meet in the European Champions League.

This book of footballing facts, feats and oddities can be read in one sitting or dipped into at will (perhaps at half-time or after the news while waiting for *Match of the Day* to begin), or it can be used as a quiz book to test the depth of your football knowledge or that of your mates.

If you do decide to use the book for quizzes, these posers will get you started:

* *Who are the only team to have won a European trophy, having been knocked out of the competition in the Second Round?*
* *Who was the last Englishman to manage a League Championship-winning side?*
* *How did Joe Gaetjens humiliate English football?*
* *Which team did a disgruntled fan sue under the Trades Description Act after a particularly poor performance?*
* *Who won a European trophy without actually scoring more goals than their opponents?*
* *Which school entered the FA Cup because the headmaster feared that the pupils were not getting enough exercise?*
* *In what year were ribbons first used to adorn the FA Cup?*
* *Who did the first football club play their matches against?*
* *Why was the first World Cup Final played with a different ball in each half?*
* *Who is the only British footballer to win an Oscar?*

ABBREVIATIONS

CCC - County Cricket Club

ECWC - European Cup Winners' Cup

FA - Football Association

FC - Football Club

Fifa - Fédération Internationale de Football Association

Uefa - Union of European Football Associations

---

* How much was the maximum wage for players when introduced in 1901?
* What unusual fate befell French World Cup captain Alex Villaplane?
* How many matches did the first Pools Panel deliberate on?

NOTE

If you would like to gauge some idea of the modern equivalents of the monetary values given in some of the earlier entries, the website http://www.measuringworth.org/datasets/ukearncpi provides helpful calculators based on various indicators such as the Retail Price Index (RIP) or the index of average earnings.

◆·•◆·•◆

THE FIRST
RECORDED FOOTBALL CLUB
SHEFFIELD FC, PARKFIELD HOUSE, HIGHFIELD, SHEFFIELD, SOUTH YORKSHIRE, ENGLAND, SATURDAY 24 OCTOBER 1857

Sheffield FC was the first football club anywhere in the world. Nathaniel Creswick and William Prest, members of a local cricket team, were the founders. Originally, the team based its headquarters in a greenhouse on East Bank Road owned by Thomas Asline Ward, the father of Frederick Ward who was the first club president. Their 'ground' was a nearby playing field. Its first competitive matches were between members of the club who divided themselves into marrieds against singles or professionals against the others. There is no record of a 'shirts v skins' game. The first laws, known as the Sheffield Rules, were formulated on 21 October 1858 and there was no mention about offsides, so forwards – then known as 'kick throughs' – would hang around the opposition goal mouth. The rules did introduce a free kick for fouls and players were also allowed to push or hit the ball with their hands. Sheffield now play in the Northern Premier League Division One South, but are actually based at the Coach and Horses Pub in Dronfield, Derbyshire.

The Football Association was formed on 26 October 1863 at a meeting at the Freemason's Tavern, Long Acre, London by representatives of Blackheath School, Barnes, Blackheath, Crystal Palace, Crusaders, Forest of Leytonstone (later to become Wanderers and the first winners of the FA Cup), Kensington School, N.N. Club (N.N. stood for No Names and they came from Kilburn), Perceval House of Blackheath, Surbiton and War Office.

No rules or laws were established at the inaugural meeting because some clubs, led by Blackheath, wanted to include rugby union in the association. On 1 December the rugby proponents were defeated in a vote by 15 to four and pulled out of the FA. The laws were enshrined on 8 December. There were no laws about how many players each side should have, so the first match played under the new rules was a 14-a-side on 9 January 1864 at Battersea Park between teams chosen by the president and secretary of the FA. The President's XIV was Arthur Pember (the president), Charles Alcock, H.W. Chambers, A.M. Tebbut, Gray, Drew, R.G. Graham, W.J.

Cutbill, Alexander Morten, J. Turner, Morris, Renshaw, Leuchers and A. Scott, while the following turned out for the Secretary's XIV: Ebenezer Morley (the secretary), J.F. Alcock, C.M. Tebbut, A. Lloyd, C. Hewitt, G.T. Wawn, J.P. Phillips, Innes, McCalmont, Needham, H. Baker, A.J. Baker, Hughes and Jackson. The President's XIV won by two goals to nil, with Charles Alcock netting both. Meanwhile, up north the Sheffield clubs, however, continued to adhere to the Sheffield Rules.

THE FIRST
RECORDED LOCAL 'DERBY'

Hallam FC v Sheffield FC at Sandygate Road, Crosspool, Sheffield, South Yorkshire, England, Boxing Day Wednesday 26 December 1860

Hallam FC, founded on 4 September 1860, have the world's oldest ground and it is the one they use to this day. It has a capacity of 1,000 (250 seated). Like Sheffield FC, Hallam FC evolved out of a local cricket team. The first derby ended in a 2-0 win for Hallam.

THE FIRST
RECORDED SCOTTISH CLUB
QUEEN'S PARK,

3 EGLINTON TERRACE, GLASGOW, LANARKSHIRE, SCOTLAND, 8.30 PM TUESDAY 9 JULY 1867

The oldest club in Scotland was created at a meeting of 'a number of gentlemen... for the purpose of forming a football club'. The club was named Queen's Park, but only after a heated debate and only by one vote. Being the first club gave them few opportunities to play, so they often played against each other to keep fit. Their first match was against the now defunct Thistle FC on 1 August 1868 and Queen's Park won 2-0. **They are currently the ONLY amateur team in the Scottish League.** The club's motto is *Ludere causa ludendi* – to play for the sake of playing.

THE FIRST

FA CUP FINAL
ROYAL ENGINEERS V WANDERERS
AT THE OVAL, KENNINGTON, SURREY, ENGLAND, SATURDAY 16 MARCH 1872

The oldest football competition in the world began on 16 October 1871 with 15 teams entering, eight of them from London: Barnes, Civil Service, Clapham Rovers, Crystal Palace (not the present team), Donington Grammar School (Lincolnshire), Hampstead Heathens, Harrow Chequers, Hitchin, Maidenhead, Marlow, Queen's Park (the only Scottish entrants), Reigate Priory, Royal Engineers, Upton Park and Wanderers. Donington Grammar School, Harrow Chequers and Reigate Priory withdrew from the competition before actually playing a game. The headmaster of Donington entered his school because he feared that his pupils were not getting enough exercise, but they were drawn against Queen's Park and could not afford the rail fare to Scotland. Wanderers reached the final having won just one game – they played Queen's Park in the Semi-Final at The Oval, Kennington, Surrey and the match ended in a draw on 5 March 1872. However, the Scottish team withdrew when they could not afford to travel to London again for the replay. Royal Engineers had beaten Crystal Palace 3-0 in the replay after a goalless Semi-Final on 17 February 1872 – both the Semis were played at The Oval.

Royal Engineers met Wanderers in the Final, admittance to which cost a shilling and there were no crossbars, nets, free kicks, penalties, centre circle or halfway line. Both teams had an abundance of forwards – Royal Engineers had seven and Wanderers eight. Charles Alcock – the Old Harrovian captain of Wanderers, secretary of the Football Association and creator of the FA Cup – won the toss and chose to defend the Harleyford Road end of the ground. This meant that the favourites Engineers had the sun and wind in their faces. With the game only ten minutes old, Lieutenant Edmund Cresswell of the Royal Engineers broke his collarbone but, with no substitutes available, refused to leave the pitch. After 15 minutes Wanderers' Morton Betts, playing under the pseudonym 'A.H. Chequer', scored what was the only goal of the game.

THE NO CUP FINAL

Wanderers didn't receive the Cup at the match, but had to wait until April 1872 when it was presented to them at a special reception at the Pall Mall Restaurant in London by FA president Ebenezer Morley. It was not until 1882 that the tradition of presenting the winners with the trophy at the end of the match began.

In those days, teams changed ends after each goal was scored. On 20 minutes Charles Alcock scored, but the goal was disallowed because Charles Wollaston had handled the ball. Wanderers continued to attack and it was only the skill of William Merriman in the Royal Engineers' goal that stopped Wanderers adding to the score.

THE FIELD CALLED THE FINAL 'the fastest and hardest match that has ever been seen at The Oval' AND WANDERERS DISPLAYED 'some of the best play, individually and collectively, that has ever been shown in an Association game'. **THE TIMES** REPORTED: 'Overall, the Royal Engineers appeared to possess the more skilled football team and offered much evidence they would emerge victorious; however, one has discovered anything may happen in this knockout-style tournament.'

OTHER FIRSTS IN THIS MATCH:

The FIRST goal in an FA Cup Final • The FIRST goal disallowed in an FA Cup Final • The FIRST clean sheet in an FA Cup Final

━•━••━

THE FIRST

INTERNATIONAL MATCH

SCOTLAND V ENGLAND AT THE WEST OF SCOTLAND CRICKET GROUND, HAMILTON CRESCENT, PEEL STREET, PARTICK, GLASGOW, LANARKSHIRE, SCOTLAND, 2.20 PM SATURDAY 30 NOVEMBER 1872

The first football international in the world was watched by around 4,000 people at a cricket ground that received £1 10s for its hire. The match, played in sunshine on a pitch that had been rained on for the previous two days, ended 0-0. Scotland's team, clad in 'dark blue shirts with a lion crest, white knickerbockers, blue and white striped stockings and red head cowls', was picked by its captain Robert W. Gardener – all of whom played for Queen's Park – and they played in a 2-2-6 formation. The Football Association picked the England side, but Charles Alcock – the Old Harrovian captain of Wanderers, secretary of the FA and creator of the FA Cup – had the most influence. He was unable to play in the inaugural match because of an injury. England, resplendent in 'white shirts with three lions crest, white knickerbockers and dark blue caps', played in a 1-2-7 formation.

A REPORT THE NEXT DAY IN **BELL'S LIFE** IN **LONDON AND SPORTING CHRONICLE** SAID: 'The only thing which saved the Scotch team from defeat, considering the powerful forward play of England, was the magnificent defensive play and tactics shown by their backs, which was also taken advantage of by the forwards...'

THIS MATCH WAS ALSO:

The ONLY occasion the Scottish team was selected from the same club

THE FIRST

GOALKEEPER TO CAPTAIN ENGLAND

ALEXANDER MORTEN, ENGLAND V SCOTLAND AT THE OVAL, KENNINGTON, SURREY, ENGLAND, 3 PM SATURDAY 8 MARCH 1873

Crystal Palace goalie Alexander Morten captained his country in his only international appearance when England beat Scotland 4-2 in England's second official international and first win. He was also the oldest debutant, being 41 years and 114 days old, and the second oldest (after Stanley Matthews) to play for England. Bizarrely, in the first friendly, unofficial international between England and Scotland on 5 March 1870, also staged at The Oval, Morten played in goal for Scotland. The match ended 1-1. Morten died in New York on 16 September 1916.

OCCASION WHEN THE FA CUP WINNERS GOT A BYE TO THE FOLLOWING YEAR'S FINAL

Wanderers v Oxford University at Lillie Bridge Amateur Athletic Ground, Lillie Road, Fulham, London, England, 11.30 am Saturday 29 March 1873

Having won the inaugural Cup the previous season, Wanderers were given a bye to the Final where they met Oxford University. As the Boat Race was being staged on the same day, the Cup Final kick-off was changed to the morning so that spectators could, if they wished, watch both events. Only 3,000 turned up to see the football. Wanderers also had the right to choose a venue and since they did not have their own picked Lillie Bridge, which was near the present-day Stamford Bridge. Oxford University had most of the play, but William Kenyon-Slaney put the ball into the net for Wanderers only for it to be disallowed because he was offside. It was after 27 minutes that Wanderers captain Hon. Arthur Kinnaird opened his team's account. Determined to equalize, Oxford University moved Andrew Leach out of goal and into attack. With ten minutes to go Charles Wollaston scored the second goal for Wanderers to retain the trophy.

THE FIRST

MATCH AT HAMPDEN PARK

QUEEN'S PARK V DUMBRECK AT HAMPDEN PARK, KINGSLEY AVENUE, GLASGOW, LANARKSHIRE, SCOTLAND, SATURDAY 25 OCTOBER 1873

The first game at Hampden Park, the home of Queen's Park, was also their first match in the Scottish FA Cup. Queen's Park won 7-0 and went on to win the trophy. Although Hampden Park has always been the home of Queen's Park, it has not been the same stadium. There have been three Hampden Parks so far with the first being occupied between 1873 and 1884. They spent 19 years at the second Hampden Park before moving into the current one where the first game was played on Hallowe'en 1903 and Queen's Park beat Celtic 1-0.

THE FIRST
RECORDED USE OF SHIN PADS
NOTTINGHAM FOREST, 1874

The first football team to wear shin pads was Nottingham Forest in 1874. The team's centre forward Sam Widdowson invented the safety measure, but he wore them outside his socks. He cut down a pair of cricket pads and was initially ridiculed by other players.

THE ONLY
SENIOR BRITISH CLUB
NAMED AFTER A SCHOOL
HAMILTON ACADEMICAL, 1874

Founded at the end of 1874, the club was formed by the rector and pupils of the local school in South Lanarkshire, Scotland, Hamilton Academy. They joined the Scottish Football League in November 1897 when Renton were forced to resign from the League after being unable to meet their financial obligations.

THE FIRST
EXTRA TIME IN AN
FA CUP FINAL
ROYAL ENGINEERS V OLD ETONIANS AT THE OVAL, KENNINGTON, SURREY, ENGLAND SATURDAY 13 MARCH 1875

Having lost the first Final and again in 1874, the Royal Engineers returned for their third attempt. The man in the middle was Charles

Alcock, who had invented the FA Cup and captained the victorious Wanderers team in the first Final. Old Etonians won the toss and chose, unsurprisingly, to play with the wind or, as the newspapers of the time reported it, the 'howling gale'. Owing to the rule of teams changing ends every time a goal was scored, Royal Engineers played into the wind for all apart from about ten minutes of the game. After 37 minutes Lieutenant Richard Ruck of the Sappers' midfield went in for a heavy tackle on Etonian inside forward Cuthbert Ottaway that resulted in him having to leave the field with an injured ankle. Despite being down to ten men, three minutes later Alexander Bonsor (who had played in the first two Finals for Wanderers) curled a corner kick into the goal to give the Old Etonians the lead. The Royal Engineers attacked and scored through Captain Henry Renny-Tailyour.

The wind made good play impossible and the match ended 1-1 after 90 minutes. Thirty minutes of extra time could not break the deadlock and the teams met again three days later at The Oval. Several Old Etonians were unable to make the replay and indeed the team arrived an hour late for the kick-off. Royal Engineers won 2-0 with goals from Lieutenant William Stafford and again from Captain Renny-Tailyour.

ANOTHER FIRST AND A LAST IN THIS MATCH:
The FIRST FA Cup Final refereed by a former finalist • The LAST FA Cup Final in which teams changed ends after every goal

THE FIRST
CROSSBAR
1875

In 1875 the crossbar was introduced to replace the tape that had previously marked the top of the goal and was itself an innovation in 1865. Both were 8 ft (2.4 m) from the ground. In 1895 it was ruled that the goalposts and crossbar could be no wider than 5 in (12.7 cm).

THE FIRST

BROTHERS FROM THE SAME CLUB

TO PLAY FOR ENGLAND

IN THE SAME MATCH

FRANK AND HUBERT HERON, ENGLAND V SCOTLAND AT HAMILTON CRESCENT, PARTICK, GLASGOW, LANARKSHIRE, SCOTLAND, SATURDAY 4 MARCH 1876

To date there have been ten sets of brothers to play for England. The first were Herbert and William Rawson in 1875, but the first from the same club were the Heron brothers who played for Wanderers. Hubert Heron played five times for his country and donned the captain's mantle once in the only game that brother Frank played in – a 3-0 defeat by Scotland. Frank, described as 'an excellent dribbler but rather too light', later became a wine merchant and died on 23 October 1914, aged 61.

THE FIRST

MATCH PLAYED UNDER

FLOODLIGHTS

Reds v Blues at Bramall Lane, Sheffield, South Yorkshire, England, Monday 14 October 1878

Floodlights – four Siemens arc-lamps on 30 ft (9 m) wooden towers in each corner of the ground – were used experimentally at Sheffield United's stadium, but they were unreliable and it would be almost 80 years before the Football League agreed to their usage in official matches. In front of nearly 20,000 spectators John (later Sir Charles) Clegg captained the Reds, who beat the Blues – captained by his brother William Clegg – by two goals to nil. (See 1956, page 102.)

THE FIRST

PLAYER TO REPRESENT ENGLAND AT FOOTBALL AND CRICKET

RT. HON. ALFRED LYTTELTON, ENGLAND V SCOTLAND AT THE OVAL, KENNINGTON, SURREY, ENGLAND, SATURDAY 3 MARCH 1877; ENGLAND V AUSTRALIA AT THE OVAL, KENNINGTON, SURREY, ENGLAND, MONDAY 6 SEPTEMBER 1880

Alfred Lyttelton (1857–1913) was the eighth son and youngest of the 12 children of the 4th Baron Lyttelton and Mary Glynne, who was William Gladstone's sister-in-law. At Eton he excelled in all sports, leading a friend to comment, 'No athlete was ever quite such an athlete, and no boyish hero was ever quite such a hero as was Alfred Lyttelton.' In 1875 he went up to Trinity College, Cambridge where he was the leading cricketer. In fact, his family was so large that they could provide a full-strength team. He played just once for England at football, scoring his country's solitary goal in a 3-1 defeat by Scotland. Having been educated at Eton, he did not lack self-confidence and went on long dribbles, much to the annoyance of his teammates, one of whom, Billy Mosforth, yelled at him. 'I play for my own pleasure,' was Lyttelton's reply. He was also amateur royal tennis champion from 1882 until 1896. Lyttelton was the Liberal Unionist MP for Warwick and Leamington from 1895 to 1906 when he lost his seat, and represented St George's Hanover Square from June 1906 until his death.

Lyttleton also played cricket for England, taking part in four Tests, and his best bowling figures were four for 19 with underarm lobs. He died on 5 July 1913, aged 56, at 3 Devonshire Terrace, Marylebone, London, a nursing home, from an abscess caused by being hit in the stomach while scoring 89 in a cricket match at Bethnal Green.

ALFRED LYTTELTON WAS ALSO:

The FIRST double international at football and cricket • The ONLY Cabinet Minster to have played football for England – he was Secretary of State for the Colonies from October 1903 to December 1905

THE FIRST
BLACK INTERNATIONAL PLAYER
ANDREW WATSON, SCOTLAND V ENGLAND AT THE OVAL,
KENNINGTON, SURREY, ENGLAND, SATURDAY 12 MARCH 1881

Born in Demerara, British Guiana on 18 May 1857, the illegitimate son of Peter Miller, a wealthy Scottish sugar plantation owner, and Rose Watson, a local woman, Andrew Watson studied at the University of Glasgow where he began playing football as a full back on either side. He signed for Queen's Park in 1880 and in the spring of the following year made his international debut against England, the first of three appearances. Scotland won them all: 6-1 against England, 5-1 against Wales (14 March 1881 at Acton Park, Wrexham) and 5-1 again against England (11 March 1882 at Hampden Park, Glasgow). He later emigrated to Australia and died in Sydney on 16 January 1902. (See 1965, page 130.)

THE FIRST
HAT-TRICK FOR ENGLAND
Howard Vaughton, England v Ireland at Knock Ground, Belfast,
Ireland, Saturday 18 February 1882

Making his international debut, Aston Villa forward Howard Vaughton was the first hat-trick scorer for England. He actually went two better and netted five in what remains England's biggest international victory as they demolished Ireland 13-0. In fact, the half-time score was 13-0, and in the second half England went easy on the beleaguered Irish and didn't add to their humiliation before 2,500 spectators. Vaughton opened his account with just three minutes on the clock and his hat-trick came in the space of just seven minutes. Vaughton's Villa teammate Arthur Brown, also making his international debut, supplied four to become England's second hat-trick scorer. They would be the only goals he would score for his country in three appearances.

THE LAST
SEASON IN WHICH PLAYERS COULD
TAKE THROW-INS ONE-HANDED
1881–1882

The two-handed throw-in was made compulsory in 1883. In 1895 it was decreed that players taking a throw-in must stand on the touchline.

THE FIRST
INTERNATIONAL FOOTBALL COMPETITION
IRELAND V SCOTLAND AT BALLYNAFEIGH PARK, ORMEAU ROAD, BELFAST, IRELAND, 3 PM THURSDAY 24 JANUARY 1884

On 6 December 1882 the Football Association, the Scottish Football Association, the Football Association of Wales and the Irish Football Association met in Manchester to formulate one set of rules for the game to be used worldwide. At the same meeting the annual tournament that became the British Home Championship was born. Scotland beat Ireland 5-0 to win the first match and went on to win the first tournament. Scotland were 2-0 up at half-time through goals by William Harrower (12 minutes) and James Gossland (30 minutes) before adding three more in the second half. Harrower (86 minutes) and Gossland (70 minutes) added to their tally and John Goudie hit the other goal on the 60th minute. Scotland's two other games in the tournament were both played at Cathkin Park, Glasgow and they beat England 1-0 on 15 March 1884 and Wales 4-1 two weeks later. Although usually winning the competition had no significance (save for national pride), in 1949–1950 and 1953–1954 the tournament was used as a qualifying group for the 1950 and 1954 World Cups. In 1966–1967 and 1967–1968 it decided who went forward to the second qualifying round of Euro '68. (See 1980–1981, page 171 and 1983–1984, page 179.)

THIS WAS ALSO:
The FIRST Home Championship match

THE ONLY
TEAM TO PLAY IN THE FA CUP
AND SCOTTISH FA CUP FINALS
IN SAME SEASON

QUEEN'S PARK, 1883-1884: FA CUP V BLACKBURN ROVERS AT THE OVAL,
KENNINGTON, SURREY, ENGLAND, SATURDAY 29 MARCH 1884; SCOTTISH
FA CUP V VALE OF LEVEN AT CATHKIN PARK, GLASGOW, LANARKSHIRE,
SCOTLAND, 3 PM SATURDAY 23 FEBRUARY 1884

Queen's Park met Blackburn Rovers before 12,000 spectators – the biggest thus far in the competition – at The Oval in the 13th FA Cup Final, but lost 2-1. All three goals were scored in the 15 minutes leading up to half-time and in the second half the Scottish team were outplayed. A month earlier they had won the Scottish FA Cup for the seventh time in a walkover beating Vale of Leven. On 4 April 1885 Queen's Park and Blackburn Rovers met in the 14th FA Cup Final at the same venue. On this occasion Queen's Park were the favourites, but the Blackburn victory was slightly more emphatic as they won 2-0. Indeed, the score was perhaps generous to Queen's Park since Herby Arthur, the Rovers goalie, only touched the ball five times during the entire match.

THE FIRST
MATCH AT ANFIELD

EVERTON V EARLESTOWN AT ANFIELD, SEAFORTH, LIVERPOOL,
LANCASHIRE, ENGLAND, SATURDAY 27 SEPTEMBER 1884

The stadium that has become synonymous with Liverpool was originally home to their deadly rivals Everton. The stadium was opened in 1884 and was owned by John Orrell, a friend of Everton's president John Houlding. His club had played at Priory Road, but were looking for a new home. John Orrell let Everton have the ground for a charitable donation to the local hospital. The first match Everton played at their new Anfield football ground was against Earlestown, who were beaten 5-0. In 1885 John

Houlding bought the land outright for £5,845 and the club began paying rent to its own president. John Orrell still owned the adjacent land. The first League match staged at Anfield was on 8 September 1888 between Everton and Accrington. Everton won 2-1 thanks to a brace from George Fleming.

In 1890–1891 Everton brought the first League Championship to Anfield. Houlding increased the rent he was charging his own club to £250 a year, but the club offered only £180. Then John Orrell announced that he wanted to build a road to his land – the only problem was that the proposed road would run through the then newly built main stand. Everton Football Club believed that their president knew what his friend was planning and having had enough of their Machiavellian president upped sticks and moved to Goodison Park, which was officially opened on 24 August 1892 by Lord Kinnaird and Frederick Wall of the FA.

Houlding was left with a stadium but no club to fill it, so he decided to create a new team. He wanted to call them Everton FC and Athletic Grounds Ltd or Everton Athletic for short, but the Football Association refused to recognize the team as Everton. Thus on 15 March 1892 Liverpool FC and Athletic Grounds Ltd was born. Their first match at Anfield was a friendly against Rotherham Town, kicking off at 5.30 pm on 1 September 1892. Two hundred spectators watched Liverpool win 7-1. The first match played by the Reds in the Football League was on 2 September 1893 away to Middlesbrough Ironopolis. Liverpool won 2-0, despite the long grass that impeded play.

THE FIRST

PROFESSIONAL
INTERNATIONAL

JAMES HENRY FORREST, ENGLAND V SCOTLAND AT THE OVAL, KENNINGTON, SURREY, ENGLAND, SATURDAY 21 MARCH 1885

Blackburn Rovers left half Jimmy Forrest became the first professional international when he was selected aged 20 for the match against Scotland in the Home Championship. A protest from the Scottish Football

Association that all international players should be amateurs went unheeded, although Forrest had to forgo his weekly £1 wage and wear a different shirt from his teammates. Forrest, who played for Blackburn between January 1883 and 1890, made 11 appearances for his country. His debut match as a professional (in fact, his fourth cap) ended in a one-all draw.

THE ONLY
FOOTBALL LEAGUE GROUND
THAT BACKS ONTO A CEMETERY

Gigg Lane, Bury, Lancashire, England, 1885

Gigg Lane, the home ground of Bury and the only Football League stadium that backs onto a cemetery, was home to its first match on 12 September 1885, a friendly against Wigan Athletic, which the home team won 4-3. Four years later, on 5 November 1889, the ground was host to a match by floodlights for the first time when Bury lost 5-4 to Heywood Central.

THE FIRST
ALL-FOREIGN
INTERNATIONAL MATCH

UNITED STATES OF AMERICA V CANADA AT NEWARK, NEW JERSEY, USA, SATURDAY 28 NOVEMBER 1885

The first football international played without involving a British side was between the USA and Canada, and the visitors won 1-0 before 2,000 spectators. However, the match was not officially recognized and **the FIRST official match involving all foreigners** was held 16 years later on 16 May 1901 between Argentina and Uruguay. The Argentines won 3-2.

THE FIRST

RECORDED
CATHOLIC PLAYER AT RANGERS

Pat Lafferty, 1886

A contentious subject – for many years there was an unwritten rule that Catholics didn't play for the mainly Protestant-supported Rangers and Protestants didn't join the mainly Roman Catholic-supported Celtic. When the Catholic Mo Johnston signed for Rangers from Nantes for £1.2 million on 10 July 1989, it was reported in newspapers as him being the first Catholic to play for the Ibrox club. In fact, more than a dozen Catholic players have donned the blue shirt of Rangers. The first was in 1886, 13 years after the club's formation, and was Pat Lafferty. Others have included: Tom Dunbar (1891–1892), J. Tutty (1899–1900), Archie Kyle (1904–1908), Willie Kivlichan (1906–1907), Colin Mainds (1906–1907), Tom Murray (1907–1908), William Brown (1912), Joe Donnachie (c. 1914–1918), John Jackson (1917), Laurie Blyth (1951–1952), Don Kichenbrand (1955–1956), Hugh O'Neill (1976) and John Spencer (1985–1992).

THE LAST

SEASON SCOTTISH TEAMS
PARTICIPATED IN THE FA CUP

1886–1887

A number of Scottish teams including Cowlairs, Heart of Midlothian, Partick Thistle, Queen's Park (the most successful, reaching the FA Cup Final in 1884 and 1885, although losing on both occasions to Blackburn Rovers), Rangers, Renton and Third Lanark had all competed in the FA Cup before the Scottish Football Association banned such participation. In the final season Cowlairs beat Darwen Old Wanderers 4-1 away in the First Round on 23 October 1886. In the Second Round on 23 November

1886 they thrashed Rossendale 10-2 away. Rangers knocked them out 3-2 away on 4 December 1886 in the Third Round. On 30 October 1886 Heart of Midlothian lost 7-1 away to Darwen in the First Round, having the original tie against Padham scratched.

Partick Thistle beat Blackburn Olympic 3-1 away in the First Round on 23 October 1886. In the Second Round, again drawn at home, they thrashed Fleetwood Rangers 7-0 on 20 November 1886. Seemingly unstoppable, they beat Cliftonville 11-0 away in the Third Round on 4 December 1886 – **the ONLY occasion when a Scottish team beat an Irish one in the FA Cup** – received a bye in the Fourth Round, but lost 1-0 away to Old Westminsters in the Fifth on 29 January 1887. On 30 October 1886 Queen's Park lost 3-0 at home to Preston North End in the First Round.

Rangers beat Everton 1-0 away in the First Round on 30 October 1886. In the Second Round they beat Church 2-1 at home on 21 November 1886. In the Third Round they beat Cowlairs 3-2 at home on 4 December 1886. They received a bye in the Fourth Round and beat Lincoln City 3-0 in the Fifth Round on 29 January 1887 at home. In the Quarter-Final they beat Old Westminsters 5-1 on 19 February 1887 at home, but were beaten 3-1 by Aston Villa in the Semi-Final at Crewe on 5 March 1887.

Renton beat Accrington South 1-0 at home in the First Round on 30 October 1886. In the Second Round on 20 November 1886 they drew 2-2 at home with Blackburn Rovers before beating them 2-0 away on 4 December 1886. In the Third Round, drawn at home to Preston North End, they lost 2-0 on 11 December 1886. On 16 October 1886 Third Lanark won their First Round match beating Higher Walton 5-0 at home, but were knocked out in the Second Round 3-2 at home by Bolton Wanderers on 13 November 1886.

THE FIRST
CLUB TO BECOME A LIMITED COMPANY
BIRMINGHAM CITY (AS SMALL HEATH), 1888

Birmingham City was founded in 1875 as Small Heath Alliance. After ten years they turned professional and in 1888 dropped the Alliance, becoming

Small Heath FC Ltd. They thus became the first team run by a board of directors. In 1892 they became one of the founder members of Division Two. Small Heath became Birmingham in March 1905 and Birmingham City in 1945.

THE FIRST
TEAM TO WIN THE FOOTBALL LEAGUE
PRESTON NORTH END, 1888–1889, 1889–1890

The Football League was formed at Anderton's Hotel, Fleet Street, London on 22 March 1888, which was an odd choice for a venue because there were no southern teams among the first 12 members who were Accrington Stanley, Aston Villa, Blackburn Rovers, Bolton Wanderers, Burnley, Derby County, Everton, Notts County, Preston North End, Stoke, West Bromwich Albion and Wolverhampton Wanderers. **The FIRST southern team to join the League** was Woolwich Arsenal in 1893. **The FIRST matches** were played on 8 September 1888. Jack Gordon of Preston North End is usually considered the scorer of **the FIRST goal in League football**, though there is some dispute about this because their opening match kicked off 45 minutes after the other matches. Full back Gershom Cox of Aston Villa scored **the FIRST own goal** in a one-all draw with local rivals Wolves. The first results on the opening day were:

BOLTON WANDERERS	3 – 6	DERBY COUNTY
EVERTON	2 – 1	ACCRINGTON STANLEY
PRESTON NORTH END	5 – 2	BURNLEY
STOKE	0 – 2	WEST BROMWICH ALBION
WOLVERHAMPTON WANDERERS	1 – 1	ASTON VILLA

On 15 September Walter Tait of Burnley scored **the FIRST hat-trick**. Having won the first League championship on 5 January 1889 and been undefeated during the season (22 games, 40 points and 74 goals), Preston beat Wolverhampton Wanderers 3-0 at The Oval on 30 March 1889 to win the FA Cup (they did not concede a goal in the competition) and thus complete the first League and FA Cup Double. The following season they

became the first team to retain their League title – they have never won the title since. In 1890–1891 they came second in the title race to Everton, who won with 29 points (out of a possible 42), the lowest points number of any champion side. Preston achieved 27 points.

OTHER FIRSTS FOR PRESTON NORTH END WERE:
The FIRST team to do the Double • The FIRST team to remain unbeaten in a League season • The FIRST team to retain the League title

THE FIRST
OCCASION ENGLAND PLAYED
TWO MATCHES ON SAME DAY
ENGLAND V WALES AT THE RACECOURSE GROUND, MOLD ROAD, WREXHAM, CLWYD, WALES, SATURDAY 15 MARCH 1890; ENGLAND V IRELAND AT BALLYNAFEIGH PARK, ORMEAU ROAD, BELFAST, IRELAND, SATURDAY 15 MARCH 1890

In an unusual move in the Home Championship in the 1890s, the Football Association decided to play competitive games against Wales and Ireland on the same day. Even more bizarrely they chose a team of professionals to play Ireland and a team of amateurs to play Wales. Watched by 5,000 spectators England won 3-1 against Wales. In the other match England comprehensively thumped Ireland 9-1 before 5,000 spectators. The FA believed the game against Scotland was more important, so used the other two games as a try-out. They repeated the experiment on 7 March 1891 and 5 March 1892. England won all six games.

THE ONLY
TIED SCOTTISH LEAGUE
CHAMPIONSHIP
1890–1891

The Scottish League began in the 1890–1891 season with the following teams: Cambuslang, Celtic, Cowlairs, Dumbarton, Heart of Midlothian,

Rangers, Renton, St Mirren, Third Lanark and Vale of Leven. Cameron of Renton scored the first goal on 16 August 1890 in a 4-1 win against Celtic. However, after four matches of the season, on 30 September 1890, Renton were suspended by the Scottish Football Association for professionalism – the teams were all amateurs, as professionalism had not yet been legalized in Scotland. Following the lifting of their suspension, Renton rejoined the League in time for the 1891–1892 season. Only Celtic and Rangers have never been relegated from the top league, and in addition to those two clubs, only Dumbarton, Heart of Midlothian and St Mirren are still extant. At the end of the season both Rangers and Dumbarton had 29 points from 13 wins, five draws and two losses. If the two had been separated on goals scored or goal difference, then the Championship would have gone to Dumbarton who scored more (61 to 58) and had a better goal difference (40 to 33). League authorities decided to separate the two with a play-off, but that ended 2-2, so the Championship was shared.

THE FIRST
PENALTY KICK IN ENGLAND
JOHN HEATH, WOLVERHAMPTON WANDERERS V ACCRINGTON STANLEY AT MOLINEUX GROUNDS, WOLVERHAMPTON, STAFFORDSHIRE, ENGLAND, MONDAY 14 SEPTEMBER 1891

It is believed that goalkeeper and businessman William McCrum invented the penalty kick in 1890 in Milford, County Armagh, Ireland. The International Football Association Board approved the idea on 2 June 1891 after the Irish Football Association presented it at the Alexandra Hotel, Bath Street, Glasgow, and the innovation was introduced in time for the 1891–1892 season. The first penalty kick was given to Wolves and John Heath stepped up to the mark and scored in a 5-0 victory. It is thought that **the FIRST penalty in Britain** was taken at Airdrieonians on 6 January 1891. McCrum died in December 1932, aged 67.

THE FIRST
TIME GOAL NETS WERE USED IN AN FA CUP FINAL

ASTON VILLA V WEST BROMWICH ALBION AT THE OVAL, KENNINGTON, SURREY, ENGLAND, SATURDAY 19 MARCH 1892

Some 25,000 spectators watched the first Final with goal nets, which was fought between two Midlands teams. West Bromwich Albion won the Cup 3-0, with goals by Jasper Geddes, Sammy Nicholls and Jack Reynolds. Civil engineer John Alexander Brodie (1858–1934) was the developer of the nets that hung on the goals and they were first used in a League match on 1 January 1890 between Bolton Wanderers and Nottingham Forest. He later claimed that goal nets were the invention of which he was most proud.

THE FIRST
TEAM TO ADD THE SUFFIX CITY TO NAME

LINCOLN, 1892

In 1892 Lincoln, who were founded in 1884 as a successor to Lincoln Rovers, became the first club to add the suffix City to their name when they turned professional and became a limited company. They played their first League game on 3 September 1892 away to Sheffield United and lost 4-2. (See 1986–1987, page 182.)

THE FIRST
FA AMATEUR CUP FINAL

OLD CARTHUSIANS V CASUALS AT ATHLETIC GROUND, RICHMOND, SURREY, ENGLAND, SATURDAY 7 APRIL 1894

A total of 62 teams entered the tenth FA Cup competition at The Oval on Saturday 9 April 1881, although four never played a match, giving walkovers to their opponents. Old Carthusians beat Old Etonians 3-0, the goals being

THE ONLY OTHER DOUBLE

The only other team to win the FA Cup and FA Amateur Cup is Wimbledon, who beat Liverpool 1-0 and Sutton United 4-2 in 1988 and 1963 respectively. However, they could not maintain the momentum of their victory against Liverpool and go on to greater success. Wimbledon were not allowed to compete in Europe the following season because of the ban on English clubs after the Heysel Stadium disaster on 29 May 1985 in which 39 spectators died and hundreds were injured at the European Cup Final between Liverpool and Juventus. The Taylor Report that recommended all-seater stadia following the Hillsborough disaster on 15 April 1989 forced them to leave their Plough Lane home after 79 years to share with Crystal Palace at Selhurst Park. The crowds did not always follow them. On 26 January 1993 they played Everton at 'home' before a mere 3,039 fans. One travelling Everton fan commented, 'I arrived at the station, asked for directions to Selhurst Park, was told to "follow the crowds" and ended up in Argos.'

scored by Edward Wynyard, Edward Hagarty Parry and William Page.

The first FA Amateur Cup Final was the result of a plea by amateur clubs for their own competition when they found that the professional teams were dominating the FA Cup. In 1892 Sheffield FC approached the Football Association and suggested that a competition be organized for amateur teams only. The club even offered to fund a trophy, but the FA refused. Realizing that it was, in fact, rather a good idea, in 1893 the FA decided to press ahead with the tournament. They asked N.L. Jackson of Corinthian FC to arrange matters and buy a £30 trophy. There were a dozen teams in the inaugural competition, all made up of old boys from public schools. Old Carthusians (former pupils of Charterhouse School) won the FA Amateur Cup, beating Casuals in the Final 2-1. Before the match kicked off there was a controversy as to whether penalties should be allowed. A spokesman for Old Carthusians told a reporter from *The Times*, 'Penalties are an unpleasant indication that our conduct and honesty is not all it should be.'

THE OLD CARTHUSIANS WERE THEREFORE:

The FIRST team to win both the FA Cup and the FA Amateur Cup

THE LAST
SENIOR ENGLISH TEAM
TO GO A SEASON WITHOUT A DRAW
DARWEN, 1896–1897

Playing in Division Two, Lancashire-based Darwen managed to go a whole season without once drawing a match. They played 30 games, and won 14 and lost 16.

THE LAST
FOOTBALL LEAGUE TEST MATCHES
1899

At the end of the 1898–1899 season, the Football League introduced automatic promotion and relegation between Divisions One and Two (Division Two had been formed in 1892) and these replaced the Test matches that had previously decided who went up and down. The Test matches were really just a forerunner of today's money-spinning play-offs that were introduced in 1986–1987.

THE FIRST
TEAM TO ADORN
THE FA CUP WITH
WINNERS' RIBBONS
TOTTENHAM HOTSPUR V SHEFFIELD UNITED AT CRYSTAL PALACE, LONDON, ENGLAND, SATURDAY 20 APRIL 1901

Sixty years before they became **the FIRST team in the 20th century to do the Double**, Spurs, then a non-League club, won the FA Cup by beating Sheffield United 3-1 at the decidedly unglamorous setting of Burnden Park, the home of Bolton Wanderers, on 27 April 1901 after a 2-2 draw at Crystal Palace a week before. Only 20,470 people turned up to watch the replay – the smallest crowd at an FA Cup Final of the whole century. At the celebration dinner, Spurs tied blue and white ribbons on the handles of the trophy.

THIS WAS ALSO:
The FIRST FA Cup final filmed by Pathé news

━●◆◆●━

THE FIRST
MAXIMUM WAGE
1901

On 20 July 1885 professional football was legalized in England, followed eight years later by Scotland, and five years after that the Professional Footballers' Association – the players' trade union – was formed to look after their interests. Three years later clubs introduced a maximum wage for players to stop them being poached by wealthier clubs. The figure was set at £4 per week, but was raised to £5 in 1910, although it is thought that only around a tenth of players were actually paid that amount. In 1920 the figure went up to £9 a week, but two years later it was reduced to £8. Despite the threat of industrial action, the clubs remained resolute and players fell into line. By 1959 the maximum wage had risen to £20 a week during the season and £17 a week in the summer.

It was thanks to the actions of a group of players led by Jimmy Hill that the maximum wage was finally abolished and Johnny Haynes of Fulham became **the FIRST £100-a-week footballer**. Ultimately, it led to the ridiculous sums of money paid to often mediocre footballers in the game today.

━●◆◆●━

THE FIRST
MANAGER TO WIN THE LEAGUE CHAMPIONSHIP
WITH TWO CLUBS
Tom Watson, 1901

In 1892 Tom Watson led Sunderland to the League title and repeated the feat the following year and again in 1895. In 1893–1894 they were runners-up. Watson left Tyneside to move to Merseyside where he took charge at Anfield on 17 August 1896. In 1901 he led Liverpool to their first League title. To date, he is one of only four men to have achieved the feat of winning the League with two clubs, Herbert Chapman (Huddersfield Town and Arsenal), Brian Clough (Derby County and Nottingham Forest) and Kenny Dalglish (Liverpool and Blackburn Rovers) being the other three. Watson died on 6 May 1915, aged 56, while still in charge at Liverpool. Bill Walker (The Wednesday and Nottingham Forest) and Herbert Chapman (Huddersfield Town and Arsenal) won the FA Cup with two different teams.

———◆•◆•◆•———

THE FIRST
ENGLAND–SCOTLAND
INTERNATIONAL PLAYED BY ALL PROFESSIONALS
SCOTLAND V ENGLAND AT IBROX PARK, 150 EDMISTON DRIVE, GLASGOW, LANARKSHIRE, SCOTLAND, 4.01 PM SATURDAY 5 APRIL 1902

Nearly 80,000 spectators arrived to watch Scotland take on England in the Home Championship international at Ibrox in 1902. It was the 32nd meeting between the two countries and the first in which all the players were professionals. At 4.01 pm a section of the West Tribune Stand, which had been designed for 35,913 spectators, gave way due to heavy rainfall the previous night and 25 fans – all Scottish bar one – were killed and almost 600 injured. The terracing was near to the top and in the panic people at the lower edge moved out onto the surrounding track and then onto the pitch, which caused the match to be held up for 18 minutes. The game was then allowed to continue. The final score was 1-1.

Rescuers found 'a scene of indescribable horror and confusion... a mass of mangled and bleeding humanity, the victims piled one above the other... enough to unman the strongest.' Twenty-one of the dead were taken to the Western Infirmary, Glasgow. Their historians noted that 'many of the fatal injuries were caused by direct impact on the wood and steel beams and trestles. Those who first reached the ground alive must then have been at hazard from suffocation.'

A fortnight later, on 19 April 1902, *The Scotsman* declared that 516 were hurt: 'dangerously injured 24, seriously injured 168, injured 153, slightly injured 171'. The official Rangers historian put the figure at 517, and 587 were said to have received compensation. A contemporary report referred to the...

> '...*surging of the human waves on the fated terracing, the sudden gap in that portion which gave way beneath the over-pressure of the crowd tossed to and fro, the wild waving of handkerchiefs for assistance by those in front and the lamentable procession of injured and dying being carried away.*'

It was said that between 200 and 300 of the spectators fell to the ground from a height of 12–15 m (40–50 ft). Examination afterwards showed that 17 joints in what is now the Broomloan stand had given way and later in 1902 the contractor who built the western terracing in 1900 was prosecuted and acquitted. The match was declared void and was replayed at Villa Park, Birmingham on 3 May 1902. All proceeds from that game, which ended 2-2, went to the Ibrox disaster fund.

THIS WAS:
The ONLY international continued after fans had died

—•••—

THE FIRST
PLAYER SOLD FOR A
FOUR-FIGURE TRANSFER FEE
ALF COMMON, SUNDERLAND TO MIDDLESBROUGH, ENGLAND, TUESDAY 14 FEBRUARY 1905

Alf Common was born at Millfield, Northumberland on 25 May 1880 and began his career with Hylton and Jarrow in north east England before he signed for Sunderland in 1900. After 18 appearances and six goals he joined Sheffield United in October 1901 for £325. He scored the first goal in the Blades' FA Cup Final win over Southampton in 1902. On 29 February 1904 he made his international debut against Wales – the first of three caps, during which time he scored two goals in his second match against Ireland on 12 March 1904. He played his last international game on 19 March 1906 against Wales. Three months later his contract expired and he refused to sign a new one. In the summer of 1904 he returned to Sunderland for a fee of £520, plus United's reserve goalkeeper Albert Lewis.

In February 1905 he became **the world's FIRST £1,000 player** when he joined Middlesbrough, where they were in dire need of 5 ft 8 in (1.72 m) Common's talents. The local paper reported, 'He should prove a valuable acquisition to the Borough, who must win five out of their remaining ten engagements to stand any chance of escaping relegation.' Common's first game was ironically against his old club on 25 February 1905 at Bramall Lane. Boro won 1-0 and Common scored the only goal of the game (albeit from the penalty spot). It was Middlesbrough's first away win in nearly two years and they survived the drop. Common even took over as captain. However, the size of the transfer fee so amazed the footballing authorities that they set up an investigation to see if anything untoward or illegal had been carried out. As it turned out, Common's transfer was legitimate business, but the investigators discovered that Middlesbrough had been paying illegal cup bonuses to players in the previous season.

In his five years at Middlesbrough, Common played 168 League games and scored 58 goals. In 1910 he signed for Woolwich Arsenal, making his debut on 1 September against Manchester United. He scored 23 goals in 80 appearances while at Manor Ground, Plumstead Marshes, Kent before being sold to Preston North End in December 1912 for £250. Common retired from football in 1914 and managed the Alma Hotel in Cockerton and then a pub in Darlington up until three years before his death on 3 April 1946, aged 65.

THE ONLY

FOOTBALL LEAGUE TEAM
WHOSE NAME BEGINS WITH FIVE CONSONANTS

Crystal Palace, Sunday 10 September 1905

The Crystal Palace team was founded by workers at the Crystal Palace in south London and began playing their home games at the FA Cup Final ground. Palace joined the Southern League Division Two in 1905–1906 and in their first season were promoted to Division One as champions. At the start of the First World War the Admiralty requisitioned the Crystal Palace and the team was forced to find a new home. They settled at Herne Hill, the home of West Norwood. In 1917 they moved to The Nest after Croydon Common went under. In 1920 Palace joined the Football League Division Three and again won promotion as champions in their first season. In 1924 they moved to Selhurst Park where they lost their first match 1-0 to Sheffield Wednesday.

THE FIRST

TEAM TO WIN THE CHAMPIONSHIP
THE YEAR AFTER PROMOTION

LIVERPOOL, 1906

Founded in 1892 and elected to the Football League in 1893 following the resignation of Bootle, Liverpool won their first League Championship in 1900–1901, although they failed to retain their form and were relegated in 1903–1904. The following season they scored 93 goals – 60 at home where they were unbeaten. They won the League in 1905–1906, thus becoming the first team to secure the Championship having been promoted the year before. They did not begin well, losing their first three matches, including a 3-1 defeat by Woolwich Arsenal in the opening game. In October 1905 they put together an unbeaten ten-game run – nine wins and a draw.

THE FIRST

OFFICIAL ENGLAND
AMATEUR INTERNATIONAL

FRANCE V ENGLAND AT PARIS, FRANCE, THURSDAY 1 NOVEMBER 1906

The amateurs of England proved too much for their Gallic counterparts, beating them 15-0. Just over a year later, on 7 December 1907, England amateurs played their first match on their own soil, beating Ireland 6-1 at White Hart Lane.

THE ONLY
MAN TO CAPTAIN ENGLAND
AT FOOTBALL AND CRICKET

R.E. FOSTER, ENGLAND V WALES AT THE RACECOURSE GROUND, MOLD ROAD, WREXHAM, CLWYD, WALES, MONDAY 3 MARCH 1902; ENGLAND V SOUTH AFRICA AT LORD'S CRICKET GROUND, ST JOHN'S WOOD, MIDDLESEX, ENGLAND, MONDAY 1 JULY 1907

Reginald Erskine 'Tip' Foster played football for Corinthians and made his international debut against Wales on 26 March 1900 in a 1-1 draw. The following year he was named as one of *Wisden's* Cricketers of the Year. He made his Test debut against Australia in Sydney in 1903–1904 and scored 287, the highest by a debutant. He assumed the captaincy of England at cricket in 1907 for the rubber against South Africa, but was unable to lead the winter tour to Australia because of business commitments. He played five times for England at football, scoring twice in his second game against Ireland at The Dell, and was captain for the last against Wales on 3 March 1902, which ended in a goalless draw before a crowd of 10,000. He played eight Tests for England. He died of diabetes on 13 May 1914, aged just 36.

THE ONLY
FA CUP FINAL
TO INSPIRE A CAR INNOVATION
Wolverhampton Wanderers v Newcastle United at Crystal Palace, London, England, 2.30 pm Saturday 25 April 1908

In April 1908, Newcastle fan Gladstone Adams drove down to Crystal Palace in his 1904 Daracq-Caron car to see the Magpies play Wolves in the FA Cup Final. Sadly for Adams, Wolves won 3-1 before 74,967 spectators. It was Newcastle's third defeat in four years. On the way back Adams had to keep stopping his car to clear slush and snow from his windscreen. The frustrating journey inspired him to invent windscreen wipers, which he patented in April 1911.

CHARITY SHIELD

QUEENS PARK RANGERS V MANCHESTER UNITED AT STAMFORD BRIDGE, FULHAM ROAD, FULHAM, LONDON, ENGLAND, MONDAY 27 APRIL 1908

The Charity (now Community) Shield is contested between the winners of the Premier League and the FA Cup, and the first such match was in 1921, replacing the Sheriff of London Charity Shield that began on 19 March 1898. The Shield, the largest ever sporting trophy standing at more than 6 ft (1.8 m) high, was played between the best professional side and the best amateur side. **The FIRST joint winners** in the first match were Sheffield United and Corinthian, and **the LAST winners** were Newcastle United in 1907 before the competition was revived in the 1930s and 1960s.

The first Charity Shield was played between the winners of the Southern League (in this instance Queens Park Rangers) and the Division One Champions (Manchester United). The first match before 12,000 spectators ended in a 1-1 draw. It took four months for a replay to be organized, again at Stamford Bridge. At 4 pm on 29 August 1908, 10,000 spectators watched the two teams in the replay in which the Red Devils triumphed, winning 4-0, with Jimmy Turnbull scoring a hat-trick and George Wall getting the remaining goal. The 1908 Charity Shield raised £1,275 for worthy causes.

THIS IS: The ONLY Charity (Community) Shield to date that has needed a replay

THE FIRST
ENGLAND INTERNATIONAL ON FOREIGN SOIL

AUSTRIA V ENGLAND AT CRICKETER PLATZ, VIENNA, AUSTRIA, SATURDAY 6 JUNE 1908

The first time England left the British Isles to play a match occurred in the summer of 1908 when they travelled to Vienna. The first game on foreign soil ended in a 6-1 victory for England. Christiaan J. Groothoff of Holland refereed as England raced into the lead before 3,500 fans through James Windridge of Chelsea on 21 minutes. Seventeen minutes later Windridge added a second. The captain Vivian Woodward of Tottenham Hotspur made it 3-0 five minutes before the break. Five minutes after the restart Wilhelm Schmieger pulled one back for the home team. On 55 minutes centre forward George Hilsdon of Chelsea made it 4-1 to the visitors, adding his second and England's fifth 15 minutes later. With five minutes on the clock Sunderland's Arthur Bridgett on his international debut hit England's sixth.

Two days later at the Hohe Warte Stadium in Vienna they again played Austria and this time won by 11 goals to one – Vivian Woodward hitting four, Francis Bradshaw a hat-trick (despite scoring three goals, he was never picked again) and Arthur Bridgett, Ben Warren, James Windridge and Jock Rutherford scoring one apiece. England then continued their continental tour, playing Hungary on 10 June 1908 at Millenaris Sporttelep, Budapest and Bohemia on 13 June 1908 at Letná Stadium, Prague, winning 7-0 and 4-0 respectively.

THE FIRST
FOREIGNER TO PLAY
IN THE FOOTBALL LEAGUE

MAX SEEBURG, TOTTENHAM HOTSPUR V HULL CITY AT ANLABY ROAD, HULL, EAST YORKSHIRE, ENGLAND, SATURDAY 26 SEPTEMBER 1908

German forward Max Seeburg signed for Spurs in May 1907 and played for the club several times in the Southern League before making his League debut in Division Two in a 1-0 defeat away to Hull. Although it turned out to be his only appearance for the Lilywhites, he also played for Chelsea, Leyton Orient, Burnley, Grimsby Town and Reading. Although Seeburg was indeed born in Germany (in 1884), his parents had emigrated to London when he was two. He was interned for several weeks at the start of the First World War. He died in 1972 at Reading.

THE FIRST

MISSED PENALTY IN AN FA CUP FINAL

CHARLIE WALLACE, ASTON VILLA V SUNDERLAND AT
CRYSTAL PALACE, LONDON, ENGLAND, SATURDAY 19 APRIL 1913

Charlie Wallace was more of a Villain than most that day when he failed to convert his spot kick, becoming the first player to miss a penalty in an FA Cup Final. In the end the miss didn't matter too much, as Villa still won the match by one goal to nil in Sunderland's first appearance in the Final with 120,081 spectators attending the match. It would not be until 1988 that another penalty would be missed in the FA Cup Final.

THE FIRST

FA CUP FINAL ATTENDED BY A REIGNING MONARCH

BURNLEY V LIVERPOOL AT CRYSTAL PALACE, LONDON, ENGLAND, 3 PM SATURDAY 25 APRIL 1914

The two northern teams met in the penultimate final before the competition was suspended for the duration of the First World War. The game – the 43rd Final since the tournament began – was played for the last time at Crystal Palace, which had hosted every final since 1895 (excluding replays). Liverpool had reached the final by beating Aston Villa 2-0 at White Hart Lane, while Burnley needed a replay to see off Sheffield United (drawing 0-0 at Old Trafford before beating them 1-0 at Goodison Park). The teams played before 72,778 spectators, which included HM King George V, the first reigning monarch to attend a Final. Bert Freeman of Burnley scored the only goal in the 57th minute to send the FA Cup to Turf Moor for the only time in the club's history. The two teams wore their usual kits: for Burnley, claret shirts with pale blue sleeves and collars, white shorts and claret stockings with a pale blue stripe at the top, while

Liverpool wore red shirts, white shorts and red stockings (they didn't change to an all-red kit until Bill Shankly became manager).

OTHER FIRSTS AND A LAST AND ONLY IN THIS MATCH:

The FIRST FA Cup Final featuring Burnley • The FIRST FA Cup Final featuring Liverpool • The LAST FA Cup Final at Crystal Palace • The ONLY time Burnley won the FA Cup

THE ONLY

FA CUP MATCH WATCHED BY NO SUPPORTERS — OFFICIALLY

Bradford City v Norwich City at Sincil Bank, Lincoln, Lincolnshire, England, Wednesday 3 March 1915

When Norwich City and Bradford City couldn't reach a result after two matches in the FA Cup Third Round, the government stepped in and ordered that the second replay be played behind closed doors so that spectators would not be distracted from important war work. Bradford won 2-0. It is believed, however, that around 1,000 supporters gained entry to watch the match.

THE FIRST

BETTING SCANDAL TO TARNISH FOOTBALL

Manchester United v Liverpool at Old Trafford, Manchester, Lancashire, England, Good Friday 2 April 1915

Long before rumours of betting syndicates in the Far East attempting to influence English football, the first betting scandal occurred on one of the holiest days in the Christian calendar. Liverpool travelled the 33 or so miles west to Old Trafford to play their fellow reds. United were fighting to avoid

SAVED BY A FIX

Despite knowing that the game was fixed, the result was allowed to stand and was enough to put Manchester United into 18th place and save them from relegation to Division Two. Chelsea, who finished 19th, were sent down instead – or at least they would have been if the League authorities had not decided to enlarge Division One and Arsenal's devious chairman Sir Henry Norris had not done some behind-the-scenes lobbying (see 1915, page 56).

relegation, while Liverpool were mid-table and with nothing to play for except their pride. The Red Devils won 2-0, with George Anderson scoring both goals. What the fans that had paid their hard-earned money to watch the game didn't realize was that the match was fixed. The referee noticed that Liverpool didn't seem to be trying very hard and even missed a penalty.

After the final whistle was blown and the fans dispersed, rumours began to surface that a large sum of money had been placed at odds of 7/1 on a 2-0 win for Manchester United. The Football Association launched an investigation and uncovered evidence that players from both teams had been involved in a fix. The guilty were named as Sandy Turnbull, Arthur Whalley and Enoch 'Knocker' West of Manchester United, and Jackie Sheldon, Tom Miller, Bob Pursell and Tom Fairfoul from Liverpool. Jackie Sheldon, who had once worn the red shirt of Manchester United before joining the Merseysiders in November 1913, masterminded the plot. Some of the players had learned of the plot and refused to have any part of it – indeed, Liverpool's Fred Pagnam said that he would try and score a goal to wreck the result. He later gave evidence against his teammates.

On 27 December 1915 all seven players were banned for life, but that didn't much matter, since the First World War had caused Division One to be suspended. Enoch West vigorously protested his innocence and even went so far as to sue the FA for libel, but lost his case. On 3 May 1917 Sandy Turnbull, who had won FA Cup winners' medals with both Manchester City and Manchester United, was killed in action at Arras, France. His body was never recovered. In 1919 when the war was over, all the players except West had their bans overturned – Turnbull's was lifted posthumously. West's remained in situ until 1945, by which time he was 59 and rather too old to play football. He died in September 1965. A campaign to grant him a posthumous pardon was rejected outright by the Football Association in 2003.

MATCH ARSENAL PLAYED
IN DIVISION TWO

ARSENAL V NOTTINGHAM FOREST AT ARSENAL STADIUM, AVENELL ROAD, HIGHBURY, LONDON, ENGLAND, SATURDAY 24 APRIL 1915

Arsenal have the longest run in the top division of any club, being ever present since 1919. The last game Arsenal played in Division Two was against Nottingham Forest and the Gunners won 7-0 – their largest win against Forest. In 1919 the Football League resumed after the First World War and John McKenna of the FA management committee suggested that Division One be expanded from 20 to 22 clubs. Arsenal seemed to have no chance of joining the elite, having finished fifth in Division Two behind Derby County, Preston North End, Barnsley and Wolverhampton Wanderers, but ahead of Birmingham City on goal average. Arsenal's goal average was 1.683, while Birmingham's was 1.590.

Chelsea and Spurs finished bottom of Division One, and it was widely expected that both clubs would gain a reprieve and be allowed to stay in the top flight. The wily Arsenal chairman Sir Henry Norris secretly canvassed every committee member (except Spurs) and suggested that Arsenal were deserving of promotion. He also said that because Arsenal were based in London, directors of other clubs visiting Highbury could take their wives to the West End, which would be so much better than dinner in Birmingham or Wolverhampton. Norris met the chairman of Chelsea and told him that his club was safe and would be in Division One. Norris said that Arsenal deserved promotion because of 'their long service to league football', ignoring the fact that Wolves had been members for longer. When the vote was taken, Arsenal received 18,

Spurs just eight, Barnsley five, Wolves four, Nottingham Forest three, Birmingham two and Hull City only one. Arsenal were back in Division One where they have been ever since, while Spurs languished in Division Two.

THE ONLY

FOOTBALL CLUB NAMED IN THE BIBLE

QUEEN OF THE SOUTH,

PALMERSTON PARK, DUMFRIES, SCOTLAND, FRIDAY 21 MARCH 1919

The market town of Dumfries was nicknamed Queen of the South by local poet David Dunbar in his 1857 General Election address. The football team was founded at a meeting in Dumfries Town Hall on 21 March 1919 and played its first game on 16 August 1919 against Nithsdale Wanderers, drawing 2-2. The first competitive match was in the Scottish Qualifying Cup against Thornhill on 6 September 1919 and finished with the teams sharing two goals. Two thousand years before St Luke had written about the team in Chapter 11, Verse 31 of his Gospel: 'And the Queen of the South shall rise up in judgement with the men of this generation and condemn them.'

THE FIRST

EVENT AT WEMBLEY

Bolton Wanderers v West Ham United at Wembley Stadium, Middlesex, England, Saturday 28 April 1923

The FA Cup Final was the first event held at Wembley, which had not been due to open until 1924 but was completed ahead of schedule (unlike its replacement). An Army battalion tested the strength of the terraces with some vigorous marching. The Football Association had not been impressed by the poor attendance at the three post-war FA Cup Finals (held at Stamford Bridge) and did not expect a big enough crowd to fill the 125,000-

capacity new stadium. They could not have been more wrong. To ensure a good atmosphere they spent money on a comprehensive advertising campaign – and it worked. Bolton brought 5,000 fans south with them. Southern supporters (not all of them Hammers) were aided by the easy public transport links and fine weather.

The gates opened at 11.30 am and fans began to flow inside the ground. At 1 pm the authorities became worried about the number of people inside and a decision was taken to close the turnstiles at 1.45 pm, even though thousands of fans were still making their way along Olympic Way to the stadium. The stewards seemed not to know what to do and there were no allocated positions in the ground, so fans just went where they wanted. Local police were mobilized, but the crowd was too numerous for them to do anything. At 2.15 pm the crowds outside took an executive decision and broke into Wembley. To avoid the crush, many of the fans inside the ground moved onto the pitch. The crowd was officially reported as 126,047, but estimates of the actual number of fans in the ground range from 150,000 to more than 300,000. The FA refunded £2,797 (10 per cent) of the total gate money to fans that had bought tickets but were unable to reach their assigned seats. Such was the density of the crowd that the Bolton coach became deadlocked a mile from the ground and the players had to make their way to Wembley on foot.

When HM King George V who was presenting the trophy arrived, the crowd struck up with an enthusiastic rendition of *God Save the King*. Mounted police were brought in to restore order and allow the match to proceed. One, PC George Scorey on his horse Billie, became the defining image of the day and gave the game its nickname 'The White Horse Final'. PC Scorey later recalled:

'As my horse picked his way onto the field, I saw nothing but a sea of heads. I thought, "We can't do it. It's impossible." But I happened to see an opening near one of the goals and the horse was very good – easing them back with his nose and tail until we got a goal line cleared. I told them in front to join hands and heave and they went back step-by-step until we reached the line. Then they sat down and we went on like that... it was mainly due to the horse. Perhaps because he was white he commanded more attention. But more than that, he seemed to understand what was required of him. The other helpful thing was the good nature of the crowd.'

The game finally got underway 45 minutes late. With just two minutes on the clock Hammers half back Jack Tresadern became caught up in the crowd after taking a throw-in and couldn't get back onto the pitch immediately. Seizing the opportunity, 24-year-old Bolton forward David Jack shot for goal and beat Ted Hufton between the West Ham sticks. An unfortunate spectator who was pressed against the goal net was hit full on by Jack's shot and knocked unconscious. After 11 minutes the crowd surged and play was held up until the police could get them off the pitch. Bolton held on until half-time. However, the number of fans prevented the players getting to their dressing rooms, so they sat in the centre circle for five minutes before starting the second half. On 53 minutes Bolton added a second through forward Jack Smith. West Ham claimed that the ball hadn't gone into the net but hit the upright and bounced out. Referee David H. Asson from Birmingham allowed the goal, saying that the ball had gone in but had bounced because it hit a spectator.

As the match progressed, the fans, realizing that Bolton would win, began to leave Wembley. West Ham captain George Kay asked the referee to abandon the game, but his opposite number Joe Smith said, 'We're doing fine, ref, we'll play until dark to finish the match if necessary.' Mr Asson blew to herald the first Wembley win for Bolton and the king presented the trophy to Joe Smith. West Ham trainer Charlie Paynter had a novel excuse for his team's defeat. He blamed Billie. 'It was that white horse thumping its big feet into the pitch that made it hopeless. Our wingers were tumbling all over the place, tripping up in great ruts and holes,' he moaned. Both teams received £6,365 from the gate money, which was £27,776. Each of the Bolton players received a gold watch for their efforts. (See 1928, page 66 and 1930, page 69.)

THIS MATCH WITNESSED:
The FIRST goal in a Wembley Cup Final

POLICEMAN'S PREFERENCE
PC Scorey actually preferred cricket to football and, despite the offers of numerous free tickets, never went to another football match. Billie died aged 20 on 15 December 1930.

FOOTBALL POOLS

1923

The first football pools were Littlewoods in 1923 founded by John Moores. Vernons arrived in 1925, Zetters in 1933 and Brittens in 1946. People began attempting to guess whether a match would be a home win, an away win, a score draw or a no-score draw. The Football League didn't receive any money from the pools companies and this rankled, so in February 1936 they withheld the fixture list until the day before the matches, claiming that they had to be altered. It took three weeks for the Football League to cave in. In July 1959 the Football League managed to copyright the details of fixtures, forcing the pools companies to agree to pay the League between them £240,000 each year for ten years for the rights to reproduce the list.

The FIRST £100,000 winner on the pools was in 1950, while **the FIRST individual million pound winner** was Elaine McDonagh of Haworth, West Yorkshire in October 1987. She had been surviving on the dole with her husband. She won £1,010,172. Perhaps the most famous pools winner was Viv Nicholson, the wife of a trainee miner from Castleford, Yorkshire, who won £152,319 on 23 September 1961. Bruce Forsyth presented the cheque from Littlewoods. She vowed to 'spend, spend, spend' and promptly did, blowing all the money in just four years. She had an autobiography published and a film made of her life. Now in her 70s, she is a devout Jehovah's Witness. The popularity of the pools diminished with the National Lottery in 1994. (See 1963, page 123.)

—◆◆◆—

MURDERED
DIVISION ONE FOOTBALLER

TOMMY BALL, SOMERVILLE COTTAGES, BRICK KILN LANE, PERRY BARR, STAFFORDSHIRE, ENGLAND, SUNDAY 11 NOVEMBER 1923

Defender Tommy Ball signed for Aston Villa from Newcastle United on 17 January 1920. Ball with his wife Beatrice moved into Brick Kiln Lane,

Perry Barr, but soon fell out with his 45-year-old neighbour and landlord George Stagg. One night Ball, 23, and his wife went to the local Church Tavern and when they returned at 10 pm Stagg was waiting for them. The two men fell into an argument and Stagg produced a rifle and shot Ball in the chest. He died on the spot. Each corner of Ball's grave was decorated with a stone football. On 19 February 1924, Stagg, a former policeman, was tried at Stafford Crown Court and claimed that the gun had gone off accidentally. The jury took one hour and 42 minutes to reject his plea and Stagg, married with four children, was sentenced to hang. His sentence was commuted on 27 March 1924 and he was released in 1945. He died on 1 February 1966, aged 87, at Highcroft Mental Hospital in Birmingham.

THE FIRST
RECORDED PRESENTATION OF THE AUTOGRAPHED BALL TO A HAT-TRICK SCORER

CHARLES BUCHAN, SUNDERLAND V BLACKBURN ROVERS AT ROKER PARK, SUNDERLAND, COUNTY DURHAM, ENGLAND, SATURDAY 17 NOVEMBER 1923

It is likely that the tradition of presenting the player who scored a hat-trick with the ball autographed by both teams began in the 1920s. The earliest recorded instance occurred at Roker Park, when centre forward Charlie Buchan received the ball after hitting three in Sunderland's 5-1 win over Blackburn Rovers in Division One before 12,000 spectators. The score at half-time was 1-1.

THE FIRST

GOAL SCORED
DIRECTLY FROM A CORNER KICK

W.H. SMITH, HUDDERSFIELD TOWN V ARSENAL AT LEEDS ROAD,
HUDDERSFIELD, WEST YORKSHIRE, ENGLAND, SATURDAY 11 OCTOBER 1924

Billy Smith of Huddersfield scored the first goal from a corner kick in his
team's 4-0 win against Arsenal. When Huddersfield came to Highbury on
St Valentine's Day 1925 they went one better and beat the Gunners 5-0
to complete an impressive double.

THE LAST

TIME A TEAM FORGOT TO
POST ITS ENTRY FORMS
FOR THE FA CUP

QUEENS PARK RANGERS, 1926–1927

It is hard to imagine that participating in the world's oldest cup
competition could escape the minds of football's backroom boys. However,
in 1926 Queens Park Rangers were unable to enter the FA Cup because
their office staff forgot to post the application forms.

OTHER MISSED POSTS

The same misfortune befell The Wednesday in 1886–1887 and
Birmingham City in 1921–1922.

THE FIRST
RADIO COMMENTARY
ARSENAL V SHEFFIELD UNITED
AT ARSENAL STADIUM, AVENELL ROAD, HIGHBURY, LONDON, ENGLAND, SATURDAY 22 JANUARY 1927

The match at Highbury between Arsenal and Sheffield United became the first game broadcast live on the wireless. Captain Henry Blythe Thornhill 'Teddy' Wakelam, who wrote three books on rugby (and a week earlier gave the first commentary on a rugger international when his only instruction was 'Don't swear'), provided the commentary on the match for the BBC, which ended in a one-all draw. As football on the wireless grew in popularity the *Radio Times* published a diagram of the pitch, to which the commentator would refer to help listeners know where the ball was. The goal area was known as square one, and when players kicked the ball back to the keeper it was back to square one, which is where it is believed the phrase originates.

THE FIRST
FA CUP FINAL AT WHICH
'ABIDE WITH ME'
WAS SUNG
ARSENAL V CARDIFF CITY AT WEMBLEY STADIUM, MIDDLESEX, ENGLAND, SATURDAY 23 APRIL 1927

The 1927 Final was watched by 91,206 fans, with the Gunners being favourites under the management of Herbert Chapman and the captaincy of Charles Buchan. Arsenal began their campaign with a 3-2 victory against Sheffield United at Bramall Lane – it was the Blades who had

TRAGIC DISMISSAL

Goal scorer Hughie Ferguson returned to Scotland in 1929 after four years at Ninian Park. He signed for Dundee, but was unable to replicate the form that had seen him score 284 goals in ten years at Motherwell and 77 at Cardiff. He became a target for the boo boys and was dropped after scoring just two goals in 17 matches. On 9 January 1930 he gassed himself, aged 31, leaving a wife and two young children.

beaten Cardiff in the Final two years earlier. The now traditional Cup Final anthem, *Abide With Me*, was first sung in 1927. Composed by the Reverend Henry Francis Lyte in 1847, he died just two months after its completion. T.P. Ratcliff and the Band of the Grenadier Guards led **the FIRST community singing**. The 1926 Final had been relayed to public halls in Manchester and Bolton, but this was the first time the match was broadcast by the BBC, featuring Arsenal director (and future manager) George Allison and Derek McCulloch (later to become the children's entertainer Uncle Mac) as commentators.

The Bluebirds' Ernie Curtis, at 19, became **the FIRST teenager to play in the FA Cup Final**. On the 74th minute Arsenal's Welsh goalie Dan Lewis seemed to have a shot from Cardiff's Scottish forward Hughie Ferguson covered, only for it to slide into the goal off his shiny new jersey. Lewis was so disconsolate that he threw away his runner-up's medal. Teammate Bob John found it and handed it back to him with the words, 'Never mind, you'll have another chance.' It was not to be and when Arsenal returned to Wembley three years later, Lewis failed a fitness test and was dropped in favour of Charlie Preedy.

OTHER FIRSTS AND AN ONLY IN THIS MATCH:

The FIRST appearance by Arsenal at Wembley • The FIRST FA Cup Final broadcast by BBC Radio • The ONLY time the FA Cup was won by a non-English side

THE LAST

ENGLAND PLAYER TO SCORE CONSECUTIVE

INTERNATIONAL HAT-TRICKS

DIXIE DEAN, ENGLAND V BELGIUM AT OSCAR BOSSAERT STADION, BRUSSELS,
BELGIUM, WEDNESDAY 11 MAY 1927; ENGLAND V LUXEMBOURG AT JEUNESSE
STADIUM, LUXEMBOURG CITY, LUXEMBOURG, SATURDAY 21 MAY 1927

Everton's William Ralph 'Dixie' Dean was the last player to score consecutive hat-tricks on international duty for England. Earning his third of 16 caps, he hit three against Belgium in a 9-1 victory before 35,000 fans. He hit England's fifth, sixth and ninth goals in the 36th, 47th and 70th minutes. Nine-nil up, England then let up and with ten minutes to go Florimond van Halme scored a consolation goal for the home side. Ten days later England moved to another of the Benelux countries and beat Luxembourg 5-2. This time England didn't manage to reach almost double figures, but still 5 ft 10 in (1.77 m) Dean managed to hit the back of the net three times in the 18th, 65th and 72nd minutes. Dean could have had a fourth – in the 79th minute England were awarded a penalty and captain Fred Kean of Sheffield Wednesday stood up to take it. He missed, but the Belgian referee Paul Putz ordered it retaken. Fearing that he would miss again, Kean asked Dean to take it – and the Everton man promptly hit the post.

━━●◆●━━

THE FIRST

KNIGHTED PLAYER

John Charles Clegg, 1927

Although Stanley Matthews was still playing when he received his gong, he was not the first man to be knighted for services to football. That honour went to John Charles Clegg, who played for England in the first official international against Scotland in 1872. In 1923 he was appointed president of the Football Association and four years later he became Sir Charles Clegg. He died on 26 June 1937, at the age of 87.

THE FIRST

TEAMS TO WEAR
NUMBERS
ON THEIR BACKS

THE WEDNESDAY V ARSENAL AT HILLSBOROUGH, OWLERTON, SHEFFIELD, SOUTH YORKSHIRE, ENGLAND; CHELSEA V SWANSEA TOWN AT STAMFORD BRIDGE, FULHAM ROAD, FULHAM, LONDON, ENGLAND, SATURDAY 25 AUGUST 1928.

Arsenal's innovative manager Herbert Chapman reasoned that if players wore numbers on their backs it would make them easier to recognize and the game would be quicker. Consequently, Arsenal wore numbers for their away 3-2 defeat against The Wednesday (they officially became Sheffield Wednesday the following summer, although they had been billed as Sheffield Wednesday prior to this), while on the same day Chelsea wore them for their match against Swansea Town in Division Two. However, the Football League frowned on the idea and the practice was abandoned after just one match. It was not until 5 June 1939 that the Football League Management Committee finally decreed at its AGM that players would wear numbers 1–11 in League matches and that the numbers would be assigned according to position.

—◆◆◆—

THE FIRST

PLAYER SOLD FOR A
FIVE-FIGURE TRANSFER FEE

David Jack, Bolton Wanderers to Arsenal, Euston Hotel, London, England, Saturday 13 October 1928

Arsenal's manager Herbert Chapman signed David Jack when Bolton fell into financial trouble. The wily Yorkshireman arranged for the negotiations to be held in the bar of the Euston Hotel in London. Bolton wanted £13,000 for the forward. Bob Wall, Chapman's assistant and later general manager and a club director, recalled:

'*We arrived at the hotel half an hour early. Chapman immediately went into the lounge bar. He called the waiter, placed two pound notes in his hand and said, "George, this is Mr Wall, my assistant. He will drink whisky and dry ginger. I will drink gin and tonic. We shall be joined by guests. They will drink whatever they like. See that our guests are given double of everything, but Mr Wall's whisky and dry ginger will contain no whisky, and my gin and tonic will contain no gin."*'

The cunning Chapman persuaded the Bolton contingent to accept £10,890 (the previous record stood at £6,750). Sir Charles Clegg, president of the Football Association, immediately issued a statement claiming that no player in the world was worth that amount of money. David Jack – **the FIRST player to score in an FA Cup Final at Wembley** and **the FIRST player to play for two different clubs in Wembley finals** – did not turn up for training on Thursday 18 October 1928, which worried trainer Tom Whittaker who feared that the club had brought a crocked player. He went round to Jack's house to find him relaxing, his feet on the mantelpiece and a cigarette in his mouth (one of 25 he smoked a day). Jack calmly explained that he was well and fit, but always had Thursdays off at Bolton.

Whittaker soon put an end to that luxury and Jack, who always arrived at the ground in spats, made his debut for Arsenal on 20 October 1928 against Newcastle United at St James' Park when the Gunners won 3-0. In his first season he was the club's top scorer with 25 goals in 31 matches. David Jack retired on 5 May 1934 after scoring 139 goals for Arsenal in 234 matches at all levels. (See 1923, see page 57 and 1930, see page 69.)

――――◆◆◆◆――――

THE FIRST

ENGLAND INTERNATIONAL DEFEAT
ON THE CONTINENT

ENGLAND V SPAIN AT ESTADIO METROPOLITANO, MADRID, SPAIN, WEDNESDAY 15 MAY 1929

Twenty-four years before they suffered their first defeat on home soil, England travelled abroad to play a series of three friendlies in six days. On 9 May they beat France 4-1 at Colombes, Paris. Two days later they thrashed Belgium 5-1 at Parc Duden, Brussels and so went into the final match against Spain brimming with confidence. Belgian Jean Langenus, who would **take charge of the FIRST World Cup Final** in 1930, was the man in the middle. England ignored the wallopings Spain had given to Portugal (5-0) and France (8-1), and their coach Fred Pentland, a 46-year-old former Middlesbrough and England player, arranged the match to begin when the sun was at its hottest. England were without Dixie Dean for the match. Gaspar Rubio opened the score for Spain after just two minutes. Winning the last of his caps, Joe Carter of West Bromwich Albion scored on 13 minutes and added a second seven minutes later.

In the second half the heat began to tell on the England players and, encouraged by 45,000 fans and a ball that bounced shoulder high on the bone-dry pitch, the Spaniards pressed forward. Birmingham City centre forward Joe Bradford scored in the 50th minute, but it was not enough to prevent England going down 4-3 to Spain.

THE ONLY
6-6 DRAW IN DIVISION ONE
LEICESTER CITY V ARSENAL
AT CITY STADIUM, FILBERT STREET, LEICESTER, LEICESTERSHIRE, ENGLAND, EASTER MONDAY 21 APRIL 1930

The highest-scoring draw in English football history at that time was a feast of goals watched by 27,241 fans towards the end of the 1929–1930 season and five days before the FA Cup Final (which Arsenal won). In a tactic that would be recognized today, Arsenal rested some players before the Final. After just two minutes David Jack had the ball in the net, only for the referee to disallow his effort for offside. Arsenal scored first through David Halliday (in his only season in the Arsenal first team), but by half-time Leicester were leading 3-1. By the 62nd minute Arsenal were 5-3 to the good. With around 11 minutes on the clock Arsenal were leading 6-5 – all the goals coming from Halliday (four) and Cliff Bastin (two) – and then Leicester equalized. Arsenal had two more chances in the final minutes, but could not convert them. Despite his four goals

Halliday did not play in either the FA Cup Final or Arsenal's last two League games and left the club soon after.

━━•••━━

THE FIRST

PLAYER TO APPEAR FOR TWO DIFFERENT FA CUP-WINNING TEAMS

David Jack, Bolton Wanderers v West Ham United at Wembley Stadium, Middlesex, England, Saturday 28 April 1923; Arsenal v Huddersfield Town at Wembley Stadium, Middlesex, England, Saturday 26 April 1930

Having scored the first goal at Wembley playing for Bolton against West Ham, Jack made history by playing for Arsenal as they won the FA Cup for the first time in their 44-year history, beating Huddersfield Town 2-0 at Wembley before 92,488 spectators. On the team bus to the game Arsenal goalie Charlie Preedy (replacing the injured and unfortunate Dan Lewis) had said to his teammates, 'I know you think I'm the worst goalkeeper in the world. I probably am, but today I'm going to play like I'm the best.' HM King George V, making his first public appearance in 18 months after an illness, watched the match. BBC commentary was by Arsenal director George Allison. (See 1923, page 57 and 1928, page 66.)

THE 1930 MATCH WAS ALSO: The FIRST FA Cup Final in which the captains – Tom Parker (for Arsenal) and Tom Wilson – led the teams out side by side, as a mark of respect to Gunners' boss Herbert Chapman who had managed both sides

━━•••━━

THE FIRST

WORLD CUP

Montevideo, Uruguay, 1930

In 1908 the Football Association managed the football competition at the London Olympics (where Great Britain won gold), and in the 1912

Stockholm Games the Swedish FA took responsibility. Two years later Fifa agreed that the Olympics football was a 'world football championship for amateurs' and consequently took charge of the 1920 (Antwerp), 1924 (Paris) and 1928 (Amsterdam) Games. On 26 May 1928 Jules Rimet, the president of Fifa, announced plans for a football tournament outside of the Olympic Games that would include professional players. Holland, Italy, Spain, Sweden and Uruguay all offered to host the first competition. All the others withdrew their offers when Uruguay, in its centenary year, said that it would not only build a new stadium but also pay the expenses of all competitors.

Every Fifa member country was invited to compete and given a deadline of 28 February 1930 to accept. Most European countries were reluctant to undertake the arduous journey to South America. The Uruguayan Football Association wrote to the FA extending an invitation to England, Ireland, Scotland and Wales, even though they were not members of Fifa at the time, having resigned in 1928 in a disagreement over payments to amateurs. The FA declined on 18 November 1929. Eventually, after some cajoling, four European teams – Belgium, France, Romania, and Yugoslavia – boarded ships to Uruguay. Newly crowned HM King Carol II handpicked the Romanian squad. Apart from the Europeans, the rest of the competitors were Argentina, Bolivia, Brazil, Chile, Mexico, Paraguay, Peru, the United States of America and Uruguay.

THIS WAS:

The ONLY World Cup that was an invitation tournament

THE FIRST

WORLD CUP GOAL

FRANCE V MEXICO AT ESTADIO POCITOS, MONTEVIDEO, URUGUAY, 3.19 PM SUNDAY 13 JULY 1930

French inside left Lucien Laurent scored the first goal in the World Cup after 19 minutes of the match against Mexico. France were three to the good before half-time. Juan Carreño (who died of appendicitis on 16 December 1940, aged just 33) pulled one back for Mexico on 70 minutes, but Andre Maschinot completed the rout with a fourth three minutes before time. Of the historic goal, Laurent remembered:

'We were playing Mexico and it was snowing, since it was winter in the southern hemisphere. One of my teammates centred the ball and I followed its path carefully, taking it on the volley with my right foot. Everyone was pleased, but we didn't all roll around on the ground – nobody realized that history was being made. A quick handshake and we got on with the game. And no bonus either; we were all amateurs in those days, right to the end.'

The Mexican Rosas brothers – Manuel and Filipe – were the first siblings to appear in a World Cup match. There were two other sets of siblings who appeared in the 1930 tournament. Juan and Mario Evaristo (Argentina) were the second set of brothers and appeared in Argentina's first and third group matches, the Semi-Final and became **the FIRST brothers to appear in a World Cup Final**. Rafael and Francisco Garza Gutiérrez (Mexico) appeared in their country's third match against Argentina on 19 July 1930. Jean Laurent, the brother of Lucien, was in France's squad, but didn't play in a match. Lucien Laurent died on 11 April 2005, aged 97.

THIS GAME ALSO WITNESSED:
The FIRST brothers to play in a World Cup match

—•◦•—

THE FIRST
WORLD CUP
SENDING-OFF

PLÁCINDO GALINDO, PERU V ROMANIA AT ESTADIO POCITOS, MONTEVIDEO, URUGUAY, MONDAY 14 JULY 1930

The first sending-off in the World Cup was that of Peruvian Plácindo Galindo in his country's opening match in the tournament. Romania won the match 3-1 before just 300 spectators, the smallest attendance for a World Cup match, no doubt due to the date being a national holiday in Uruguay.

THE FIRST
WORLD CUP HAT-TRICK

BERT PATENAUDE, UNITED STATES OF AMERICA V PARAGUAY AT ESTADIO PARQUE CENTRALE, MONTEVIDEO, URUGUAY, 2.45 PM THURSDAY 17 JULY 1930

The USA surprised many by their performance in the first World Cup, winning both their group matches comfortably (against Belgium and Paraguay) 3-0. It was in the second of these that 20-year-old Bert Patenaude, born in Fall River, Massachusetts, hit the World Cup's first hat-trick, scoring in the 10th, 15th and 50th minutes. It was not until 10 November 2006 – 22 years after his death – that he was finally credited with the first hat-trick, as for many years it was assumed that his first had actually been a Paraguayan own goal. Patenaude played just four internationals for his country and scored six goals in those games. In the American Soccer League between 1928 and 1931 Patenaude scored 114 goals in 158 League games. He died on his 65th birthday.

THE FIRST
WORLD CUP PENALTY

MEXICO V ARGENTINA AT ESTADIO CENTENARIO, MONTEVIDEO, URUGUAY, 2.45 PM SATURDAY 19 JULY 1930

Guillermo Stábile opened the scoring for tournament favourites Argentina after eight minutes, with 28-year-old Adolfo Zumelzú adding a second four minutes later. Three minutes before half-time 17-year-old Manuel Rosas became the youngest scorer in the World Cup when he converted the competition's first penalty, and that was the way the scores stayed at 45 minutes. In the second half Argentina's superiority began to show, and despite a second from Manuel Rosas and another from Roberto Gayón, Argentina ran out 6-3 winners and with Stábile scoring a hat-trick on his international debut.

THE MATCH WAS ALSO: Unique in that five penalties were awarded, and Fernando Paternoster of Argentina became the FIRST player to miss a penalty in a World Cup.

THE FIRST

WORLD CUP FINAL

Uruguay v Argentina at Estadio Centenario, Montevideo, Uruguay,
3.30 pm Wednesday 30 July 1930

The first World Cup Final was a repeat of the 1928 Olympic football final, which Uruguay won 2-1 in a replay. The gates to the Estadio Centenario were opened at 8 am and by noon the ground was full. Soldiers stood by, bayonets fixed, and Argentine supporters were searched at the stadium entrance for hidden guns. Even before the match kicked off there was a controversy. At the time Argentina and Uruguay played their football with different-sized balls. Neither team would agree to using the other's ball, so a compromise was reached – in the first half an Argentine ball would be used and replaced with a Uruguayan version in the second 45 minutes. The referee was Belgian Jean Langenus, who feared for his safety and only agreed to officiate if there was a boat ready at the harbour to whisk him away. Both teams wore the same colour shorts and socks – royal blue – which probably made his job even harder. Argentine centre half Luis Monti received a death threat, but played anyway.

Pablo Dorado opened the scoring for the host nation, but by half-time the Argentines led 2-1 with goals from Carlos Peucelle (20 minutes) and Guillermo Stábile (37 minutes) – his eighth in the competition; he was top scorer. In the second half, playing with their own ball, Uruguay fought back and Pedro Cea scored on 57 minutes. They took the lead through Santos Iriarte after 68 minutes and put the game beyond doubt with a fourth in the 89th minute from centre forward Héctor Castro, who had also scored **the FIRST goal for Uruguay in the World Cup**. He had managed to amputate his right hand with a chainsaw when he was 13, which gave rise to his nickname El Manco, 'The Crippled'. A national holiday was declared for 31 July in Uruguay, while the Uruguayan consulate in Buenos Aires was stoned by an angry mob.

THIS WAS ALSO:

The ONLY World Cup match that used a
different-sized ball in each half

THE FIRST

SCOTLAND INTERNATIONAL DEFEAT
ON THE CONTINENT

SCOTLAND V AUSTRIA AT HOHE WARTE STADIUM, VIENNA, AUSTRIA, SATURDAY 16 MAY 1931

Scotland's first defeat on the Continent was more of a thrashing than a loss. They went down 5-0 to Austria before 45,000 spectators.

THE ONLY.

TEAM TO DATE TO WIN
THE FA CUP AND PROMOTION
IN THE SAME SEASON

WEST BROMWICH ALBION, 1930–1931

The Division Two Baggies from The Hawthorns played Birmingham City from Division One in the FA Cup Final on 25 April 1931 at Wembley Stadium. It was the 56th FA Cup Final and the ninth played at Wembley. West Brom had won the trophy twice in seven visits, while their local rivals were making their first appearance. Demand for tickets far exceeded supply. West Brom received 80,000 ticket applications from supporters, but their allocation was just 7,500. The Baggies won 2-1, with both goals scored by centre forward Billy Richardson. The *Birmingham Mail* produced a special edition of their Saturday sports paper, *Sports Argus*, which printed its match report on blue paper instead of the normal pink. It would not be until Sunderland in 1973 that a team from outside the top division won the FA Cup. West Brom's season was not over with the final – they had two League fixtures to play. They beat Stoke City 1-0 away midweek before beating Charlton Athletic 3-2 at home on the following Saturday to win promotion to Division One.

THE ONLY

PLAYER TO DIE
AS A RESULT OF AN OLD FIRM MATCH

JOHN THOMSON, CELTIC V RANGERS AT IBROX PARK, 150 EDMISTON DRIVE, GLASGOW, LANARKSHIRE, SCOTLAND, SATURDAY 5 SEPTEMBER 1931

John Thomson signed for Celtic in 1926 and took over goalkeeping duties the following year. A brave if sometimes reckless keeper, he caused one reporter to comment, 'I have no reason to change the opinion I first formed of young Thomson, the Celtic goalkeeper. Barring accident, he will one day play for his country.' On 5 February 1930 against Airdrie came the accident. Diving at an opponent's feet, Thomson broke his jaw, fractured several ribs, damaged his collarbone and lost two teeth. His mother claimed that she had had a premonition of his death and begged him to stop playing. On 16 May he was sufficiently recovered to make his international debut against France in a 2-0 win – the first of four caps. He won two Scottish Cup winners' medals with Celtic, his only club honours.

On 5 September 1931 Celtic made the short journey to Ibrox to play the Old Firm derby before 80,000 spectators. Not long after the start of the second half Rangers attacked and Sam English headed for goal. The brave Thomson rushed out to get the ball and dived at English's feet. His head hit the forward's knee, the impact fracturing his skull and rupturing an artery in his right temple. Thomson was stretchered off the field. According to *The Scotsman* the goalie was 'seen to rise on the stretcher and look towards the goal and the spot where the accident happened'. The match continued and ended in a goalless draw. Meanwhile, Thomson was taken to the Victoria Infirmary in Glasgow where at 5 pm he suffered a major convulsion. The bones of his skull pressed 5 cm (2 in) into his head where English's knee had caught him. Surgeon Norman Davidson carried out an operation to try and reduce the swelling in Thomson's brain, but without success, and at 9.25 pm the footballer was pronounced dead. He was just 22. Thirty thousand people attended his funeral four days later.

DEATH BETWEEN THE POSTS

John Thomson is the only goalie to die as a result of an Old Firm match, but he is not the only goalkeeper to die in Scottish football. On 12 November 1921 Dumbarton goalie James Williamson died as a result of an accident during a match, ironically also against Rangers.

THE FIRST

TEAM TO RESIGN
FROM THE FOOTBALL LEAGUE
Wigan Borough, Monday 26 October 1931

Wigan Borough was formed in 1920 as Wigan Association and changed their name to avoid confusion with the local rugby team. They joined the Football League Division Three North in the 1921–1922 season. Their first match as a League club was on 4 May 1921 at home to Arsenal and Wigan won 2-1. They also won their first League match (against Nelson) by the same margin. They finished 17th (of 20) in their inaugural season. However, the economy and poor performances meant that the club never achieved success. After just six matches of the 1931–1932 season Wigan Borough were forced to leave the Football League because of 'extreme financial difficulty'. Their results were expunged from the record books.

THE FIRST
TEAM TO SCORE FIRST IN AN FA CUP FINAL
AND STILL LOSE
ARSENAL V NEWCASTLE UNITED AT WEMBLEY STADIUM, MIDDLESEX, ENGLAND, SATURDAY 23 APRIL 1932

A grand total of 92,298 fans watched Arsenal's third visit to Wembley for the FA Cup Final. Bob John opened the scoring for the Gunners with a header after 15 minutes, but Newcastle United hit the back of the Arsenal net twice, the first in controversial circumstances. With seven minutes remaining in the first half, Jimmy Richardson of the Magpies chased a long pass and took the ball over the Arsenal dead ball line. The Gunners waited for the linesman to signal for a goal kick, but he kept his flag down. Richardson crossed the ball and Jack Allen equalized with a header. The referee, Percy Harper, allowed the goal to stand, even though he was unsighted more than 20 yd (18 m) from the incident. *The Times* called it 'the most controversial goal in English football history'. Newsreels later showed that the ball was out and the goal should have been disallowed. The man in black said:

'It was definitely a goal. I was so certain... that I did not even consider it necessary to consult the linesman... Whatever the film may appear to show will not make me alter my opinion.'

After 72 minutes Allen scored a second and the Cup was on its way to Tyneside.

━━━◆•◆•◆━━━

THE ONLY
FOOTBALL CLUB TO HAVE AN
UNDERGROUND STATION
NAMED AFTER IT

ARSENAL, PICCADILLY LINE, LONDON, ENGLAND, SATURDAY 5 NOVEMBER 1932

When Herbert Chapman became manager of Arsenal on 11 June 1925, few could have realized the effect he would have on the club and the football world. Among his many innovations was that he persuaded the London Electric Railway to change the name of Gillespie Road Tube Station to Arsenal. The change was worth millions in free publicity to the club and cost a small fortune in reprinting Tube maps and tickets. Chapman told the London Electric Railway that the change would encourage more people to use the Tube and thus boost revenues. Arsenal celebrated the change with a resounding 7-1 win over Wolverhampton Wanderers at Molineux.

THE FIRST

MATCH IN WHICH ARSENAL WORE RED SHIRTS WITH WHITE SLEEVES

ARSENAL V LIVERPOOL AT ARSENAL STADIUM, AVENELL ROAD,
HIGHBURY, LONDON, ENGLAND, SATURDAY 4 MARCH 1933

How Arsenal came to wear their distinctive colours is open to debate. One
theory has it that manager Herbert Chapman saw his golfing partner
cartoonist Tom Webster on the course one day with a red tank top over a
white shirt and was impressed by how much he stood out – or was he
inspired by seeing a man in that outfit on the terraces at Highbury? Up
until that time Arsenal wore plain red shirts, the first kit having been
donated by Nottingham Forest. The first match in the new kit was not a
happy experience – Arsenal lost by a solitary goal to Liverpool.

THE FIRST

FA CUP FINAL WHERE THE PLAYERS, INCLUDING GOALKEEPERS, WORE NUMBERED SHIRTS

EVERTON V MANCHESTER CITY AT WEMBLEY STADIUM,
MIDDLESEX, ENGLAND, SATURDAY 29 APRIL 1933

Everton beat Manchester City 3-0 in the first FA Cup Final in which the
players wore numbered shirts. Everton, beginning with goalie Ted Sagar,
wore numbers 1–11, while City wore 12–22, but the Mancunians began
with winger Eric Brook at 12 and ended with goalie Len Langford
donning the number 22 shirt.

THE ONLY
WORLD CUP WINNERS
NOT TO DEFEND THEIR TITLE
URUGUAY, ITALY, SUNDAY 27 MAY 1934

On 8 October 1932 Italy was chosen to host the second World Cup. Many were worried that fascist dictator Benito Mussolini would use the event as a propaganda tool. Uruguay became the first and only country not to defend the title that they won at home in 1930 because of internal problems and annoyance at the lack of European teams in the first competition.

THE FIRST
PLAYER SENT OFF
IN WORLD CUP FINALS
IMRE MARKOS, HUNGARY V AUSTRIA, STADIO LITTORIALE,
BOLOGNA, ITALY, 4.30 PM THURSDAY 31 MAY 1934

It was the Quarter-Finals of the second World Cup before a player was sent off. The player who got his marching orders was Imre Markos of Hungary in the 63rd minute. His dismissal didn't make too much difference, as the score was 2-1 to Austria at the time and stayed that way at the full-time whistle.

THE FIRST
PLAYER TO REPRESENT
TWO COUNTRIES
IN WORLD CUP FINALS
Luis Monti, Argentina in 1930; Italy in 1934

Born in Buenos Aires, Argentina on 15 May 1901, Luis Monti joined Huracán in 1921, but stayed only a year before signing with Boca Juniors and left without playing a game. He joined San Lorenzo and first played internationally in 1924, winning a silver medal at the 1928 Olympics. In 1930 centre half Monti played for Argentina in the first World Cup, scoring two goals on the way to the Final and being criticized for his often brutal tackling. He received a death threat before the Final against Uruguay, which Argentina lost. The following year he signed for Juventus and played 225 matches and scored 19 goals in Serie A. He also began playing for the Italian national side and in 1934 became the first player to appear in two World Cup Finals for different countries. He was on the winning side as Italy beat Czechoslovakia 2-1. He won 16 caps for Argentina, scoring five goals, and 18 caps for Italy, hitting the net once. He died on 9 September 1983, aged 82.

—•••◆•••—

THE FIRST
EXTRA TIME
IN A WORLD CUP FINAL
Czechoslovakia v Italy at Stadio Nazionale del Partito Nazionale Fascista, Rome, Italy, 5 pm Sunday 10 June 1934

The Czechs were captained by František Plánička (1904–1996), while Gianpero Combi (1902–1956) led the Italians. Plánička played much of his career at Slavia Prague and made 73 international appearances for Czechoslovakia, leading the team on 37 occasions. He was **the LAST surviving member of the team**. Combi spent his entire career at Juventus and made 367 appearances between 1921 and 1934. The two goalies kept clean sheets in the first half, but in the 71st minute forward Antonín Puč opened Czechoslovakia's account. Ten minutes later Raimundo Orsi, one of five attacking players in the Italian line-up, equalized and the game went to extra time. The noise was so great inside the stadium that Italian manager Vittorio Pozzo was forced to run the touchline (now illegal, of course) so that his players could hear his orders. Finally, with five minutes of extra time gone, forward Angelo Schiavio scored the winning goal. Combi, who had been beaten just three times in the competition, was presented with the Jules Rimet Trophy by the Italian dictator Benito Mussolini. In 1982 Dino Zoff became the second goalkeeper to captain a World Cup-winning team. (See 1938, page 84.)

THIS WAS ALSO: The ONLY World Cup Final in which the teams were captained by goalkeepers

THE LAST

AMATEUR TO PLAY FOR ENGLAND

BERNARD JOY, ENGLAND V BELGIUM AT STADE DU HEYSEL, BRUSSELS, BELGIUM, SATURDAY 9 MAY 1936

Born in Fulham, south west London, Bernard Joy became club captain of Casuals after graduating from the University of London. He led them to victory in the 1936 FA Amateur Cup Final and was also captain of the Great Britain football side at the 1936 Berlin Olympics. Although still registered as a Casuals player, he appeared for other teams and in May 1935 signed for Arsenal, where he deputized for Herbie Roberts. Joy made his Arsenal first team debut on 1 April 1936 against Bolton Wanderers. Just over a month later, on 9 May, he became the last amateur to play for England in their 3-2 defeat by Belgium – one of three debutants that day. Along with fellow first-timer James Cunliffe of Everton, it would be Joy's only cap. During the Second World War Joy enlisted in the Royal Air Force, but remained on Arsenal's books, playing more than 200 wartime matches for the Gunners, and won an unofficial wartime England cap. He retired not long after the war and became a football journalist and author of one of the first histories of Arsenal, *Forward, Arsenal!* (1952). He died on 18 July 1984, aged 72.

THE FIRST

LEAGUE MATCH HIGHLIGHTS BROADCAST ON TELEVISION

ARSENAL V EVERTON AT ARSENAL STADIUM, AVENELL ROAD, HIGHBURY, LONDON, ENGLAND, SATURDAY 29 AUGUST 1936

Highlights from Arsenal's 3-2 win in the opening game of the season were the first shown on television, on the BBC – the only channel at the time. Only around 1,000 people saw the game on television.

THE FIRST

ALL-TICKET
MATCH IN SCOTLAND

SCOTLAND V ENGLAND AT HAMPDEN PARK, MOUNT FLORIDA, GLASGOW, LANARKSHIRE, SCOTLAND, SATURDAY 17 APRIL 1937

The sixth and final match in the 1936–1937 Home Championship was between the auld enemies and was the first match north of the border to be an all-ticket affair. Sources for the total attendance figure vary, but more than 149,500 people attended – the largest number to watch an international in Europe – with another 10,000 watching the game free when an exit was forced open. Scotland easily won the match 3-1, but the tournament (which unusually had begun the previous October) was won by Wales, who won all three of their matches.

THIS WAS ALSO: The FIRST international match in which both teams wore numbered shirts

THE FIRST

FULL LIVE BROADCAST
OF AN FA CUP FINAL
ON THE RADIO

PRESTON NORTH END V SUNDERLAND AT WEMBLEY STADIUM, MIDDLESEX, ENGLAND, SATURDAY 1 MAY 1937

The FA Cup Final between Preston North End and Sunderland was the first Final broadcast live in its entirety on the radio. Sunderland won 3-1 and the teams had more Scotsmen playing than Englishmen – 12 to 10 (plus Sunderland's manager also being from north of the border), with Preston fielding at right half a chap called Bill Shankly.

THIS MATCH WAS ALSO: The FIRST FA Cup Final shown on television, as the BBC showed limited highlights

THE FIRST
MATCH BROADCAST LIVE
ON TELEVISION

Arsenal v Arsenal Reserves at Arsenal Stadium, Avenell Road,
Highbury, London, England, Thursday 16 September 1937

The first match that was broadcast live on television was an exhibition
match on the BBC staged between Arsenal's first team and the club's
reserve side. Unfortunately, few people watched it because most didn't have
televisions in their homes.

THE ONLY
TEAM TO WIN THE LEAGUE TITLE
AND BE RELEGATED NEXT SEASON
Manchester City, 1937–1938

The Sky Blues of Maine Road won the Division One title in 1936–1937
with 57 points, three more than second-placed Charlton Athletic and five
more than third-placed Arsenal. City scored 107 goals in their 42 matches,
almost double Charlton's 58. The following season Arsenal won the title
race with 52 points and City finished one from the bottom with 36
points, although they scored 80 goals – more than any other team in
Division One. (See 1957–1958, page 110.)

THE ONLY
NON-TOP FLIGHT SCOTTISH CLUB
TO WIN THE SCOTTISH FA CUP

EAST FIFE V KILMARNOCK AT HAMPDEN PARK, MOUNT FLORIDA,
GLASGOW, LANARKSHIRE, SCOTLAND, WEDNESDAY 27 APRIL 1938

In 1938 East Fife became the only club to date from outside the top flight
to win the Scottish FA Cup. The Division Two side drew 1-1 with

Kilmarnock in the first match at Hampden Park before 80,091 spectators and then beat them 4-2 in the replay four days later, also at Hampden Park, but before an even bigger audience of 92,716 fans.

THE FIRST
EXTRA TIME
AT A WEMBLEY FA CUP FINAL

PRESTON NORTH END V HUDDERSFIELD TOWN AT WEMBLEY STADIUM, MIDDLESEX, ENGLAND, SATURDAY 30 APRIL 1938

The 63rd FA Cup Final and the 16th held at Wembley was the first to go to extra time when Preston North End and Huddersfield Town were unable to break the deadlock in 90 minutes. Indeed, the deadlock was only broken in the final seconds of extra time when George Mutch of Preston stood up to score a penalty. Such was the lack of time that the match was unable to be restarted and Preston ran out 1-0 winners (See 1934, page 80).

OTHER FIRSTS IN THIS MATCH:
**The FIRST penalty awarded in a Wembley FA Cup Final
The FIRST FA Cup Final shown on television in its entirety,
watched by around 10,000 people**

THE FIRST
TRIPLE SENDING OFF
IN THE WORLD CUP FINALS

CZECHOSLOVAKIA V BRAZIL AT MUNICIPAL PARC LESCURE, BORDEAUX, FRANCE, 5 PM SUNDAY 12 JUNE 1938

Having been runners-up in 1934, Czechoslovakia were determined to win the World Cup in 1938, but it was not to be. They won their first game (after extra time) 3-0 against Holland and moved onto the Quarter-Finals against Brazil in an especially violent game that became known as the Battle of Bordeaux. It was the first match played at the stadium. Brazilian Zezé Procópio was sent off in the 14th minute for a vicious kick at Oldřich Nejedlý. Sixteen minutes later Leoñidas da Silva opened the scoring for Brazil (one of seven goals he would score in the tournament in which he was the top scorer), although he was likely offside. Just before half-time Arthur Machado of Brazil and Jan Riha of Czechoslovakia were caught in a brawl by the Hungarian referee Paul van Hertzka and sent off. Oldřich Nejedlý equalized from the penalty spot after 65 minutes following Domingo da Guia's handling of the ball well within the Brazilian penalty box. Then Nejedlý broke his leg during a fierce tackle. Czechoslovakia's goalkeeper and captain František Plánička suffered a broken arm after colliding with Brazil's striker Perácio's foot as the Brazilian attempted to shoot. Bravely, Plánička stayed between the sticks. The Czechs held on for 1-1, but lost the less fiercely contested replay 2-1. (See 1934, see page 79.)

THE FIRST

COUNTRY TO RETAIN
THE WORLD CUP

ITALY V HUNGARY AT STADES COLOMB, PARIS, FRANCE, SUNDAY 19 JUNE 1938

The third World Cup Final was won by Italy who beat Hungary 4-2, albeit with an almost totally new team – there were just two survivors of the team that had won the Jules Rimet Trophy in 1934. They were 27-year-old midfielder Giuseppe Meazza and 30-year-old striker Giovanni Ferrari, who became **the First players to win two World Cup winners' medals**.

THE FIRST
CHINAMAN TO PLAY
FOR ENGLAND
FRANK SOO, ENGLAND V WALES AT NINIAN PARK, CARDIFF, GLAMORGAN, WALES, SATURDAY 9 MAY 1942

Born at Buxton, Derbyshire on 8 March 1914, Frank Soo had a Chinese father and an English mother. An inside forward of some skill, he excelled in the pre-war Stoke City that also featured Stanley Matthews and Neil Franklin. During the Second World War he guested for Everton and played nine times for England between 1942 and 1945. Soo played 173 League games for Stoke and 71 for Luton Town. He died on 25 January 1991. **The FIRST black player to play for England** was Viv Anderson on 29 November 1978 in a match against Czechoslovakia. (See 1965, page 130.)

FRANK SOO WAS ALSO:
The ONLY Chinaman to play for England

THE ONLY
WORLD CUP CAPTAIN
EXECUTED FOR COLLABORATION
ALEX VILLAPLANE, FORT DE MONTROUGE, ARCUEIL, FRANCE, BOXING DAY TUESDAY 26 DECEMBER 1944

Alex Villaplane was born at Constantine, Algeria on 12 September 1905 and began his footballing career with FC Sète in 1921 after he moved to the coast to live with his uncles. He stayed at the club for three years, where his talent was recognized by the Scottish manager Victor Gibson. He was signed by Nîmes Olympique, and despite there being no professional football in France, clubs managed to get round that by paying players for spurious jobs. It was at Nîmes that he came to nationwide attention as a tough tackler, the best header of the ball in France and one of the most perceptive passers of his generation. He was **the FIRST North African** to play for France and made 25 appearances, the first against Belgium in 1926. He was appointed captain just before the first World Cup. Leading France out against Mexico on 13 July 1930 at Montevideo was, he said, 'the happiest day of my life'. France won 4-1.

A year before he had joined Racing Club de France who were trying to become the biggest club in France. Although supposedly an amateur, Villaplane made no secret of the fact that he was paid generously and spent much of his money in bars, cabarets and, most of all, on horse racing. He also began fraternizing with underworld figures.

Professionalism was legalized in time for the 1932–1933 season and he joined FC Antibes. At the time the championship was split into northern and southern halves and the winners of each played for the title. Antibes won the southern section and then beat SC Fives Lille in the play-off. It was discovered that the match had been fixed. Antibes were stripped of their title and the team's manager banned, although many believed that he was unaware of what had happened. Villaplane and two teammates with whom he had played at Sète were thought to be the real villains, but no action was taken against them.

For the 1933–1934 season Villaplane signed for OGC Nice, but he had lost much of his interest in his career, preferring to spend time watching horse races. He was fined for missing training on several occasions and was unfit when he did play. He made one last attempt to resurrect his career with the Bordeaux second division club Hispano-Bastidienne de Bordeaux in 1934–1935, managed by his old mentor Victor Gibson. Even he lost patience and sacked Villaplane after three months. In 1935 he was jailed for his part in a horse race-fixing scandal in Paris and the Côte d'Azur.

During the Second World War Henri Lafont, a local spiv turned informant and black marketeer, recruited Villaplane, by now a gold smuggler, along with others including Pierre Bonny, a once celebrated, but corrupt policeman, and the gang became known as the French Gestapo with headquarters at 93 rue Lauriston, Paris. The gang collaborated with the Germans, but also enriched themselves in the process. They were given SS uniforms and in the cellar of 93 rue Lauriston tortured and killed Jews, resistance fighters and anyone else deemed an enemy of the Third Reich.

In February 1944 Villaplane became SS sub-lieutenant in the Brigade Nord Africain (BNA), which was formed to 'cleanse' the Périgord region, and was nicknamed SS Mohammed. Villaplane's brigade was celebrated for its cruelty. When it became apparent that Germany would not win the war, Villaplane began to plot his exit. He let people escape and began to let it be known that he was only working with the Germans to help his fellow countrymen. He was arrested and put on trial. The prosecutor said:

'His psychology was different to that of the other gang members. He himself admits he is a schemer. I would say, having studied his file, that he is a conman, a born conman. Conmen have a sense that is indispensable to their trade: the sense for putting on a show. This is necessary for blinding their victims and getting them to give up what they want. He used it to commit the worst form of blackmail – the blackmailing of hope. [A witness described him] arriving in a village in a German car and wailing the following: "Oh, in what times we live! Oh, ours is a terrible era! To what harsh extremes I am reduced, me, a Frenchman compelled to wear a German uniform! Have you seen, my brave people, what terrible atrocities these savages have committed? I cannot be held responsible for them, I am not their master. They are going to kill you. But I will try to save you at the risk of my own life. I've already saved many people. Fifty-four, to be precise. You will be the 55th. If you give me FF400,000."'

Found guilty, he was sentenced to death on 1 December 1944 for his part in ten killings. He was shot by a French Resistance firing squad on Boxing Day 1944 along with Lafont, Bonny and five others.

THE ONLY
FA CUP TIE PLAYED
AFTER FANS HAD DIED
BOLTON WANDERERS V STOKE CITY AT BURNDEN PARK, BOLTON, LANCASHIRE, ENGLAND, SATURDAY 9 MARCH 1946

In 1945–1946 **the FA Cup was played over two legs for the ONLY time** from the First Round to the Sixth Round. It was the Sixth Round tie, Second Leg, between Bolton and Stoke that resulted in a tragedy at Burnden Park. Bolton won the First Leg at Victoria Ground by two goals to nil, but when Stoke visited Bolton's ground disaster struck. Shortly before kick-off 33 people were crushed to death and 400 injured following the collapse of a wall at the Railway End of the ground. The disaster was the worst to hit British football until the Ibrox deaths of 1971.

THE FIRST
FA CUP FINAL
DURING WHICH THE BALL BURST
CHARLTON ATHLETIC V DERBY COUNTY AT WEMBLEY STADIUM,
MIDDLESEX, ENGLAND, 3 PM SATURDAY 27 APRIL 1946

The Addicks met the Rams in the first post-war final before 98,000 spectators (the first time Derby had made an FA Cup Final since 1903) and for 85 minutes both teams failed to score. Then Charlton right half Bert Turner in trying to clear a shot from Derby outside left Dally Duncan managed to put the ball into his own net. A minute later Turner succeeded in putting the ball in the opposition net. He took a free kick from the edge of the box, and although County goalie Vic Woodley appeared to have the ball covered, it deflected off a defender and ended in the opposite corner. Turner thus became the first player to score for both sides in an FA Cup Final, a feat repeated by Tommy Hutchison in 1981 and Gary Mabbutt in 1987. At the age of 36 years and 312 days, Turner also became the oldest player to score in an FA Cup Final.

Towards the end of normal time Derby centre forward Jackie Stamps took a shot at goal and the ball burst. Referee Eddie Smith of Cumberland blew the whistle on 90 minutes to signal an additional 30 minutes of extra time. Derby were too much for their south London rivals and went 2-1 into the lead after just two minutes of extra time through Peter Doherty. On 97 and 106 minutes Jackie Stamps scored to make the final score 4-1 to Derby County, their solitary win in the FA Cup, although they were runners-up in 1898 and 1899. In 1968–1969 Derby County introduced an award for the supporters' player of the year and the trophy was named for two-goal hero Jackie Stamps. The first winner was Roy McFarland.

CHARLTON'S EXPLOSIVE RECORD

Amazingly, the two teams had met in the League a week earlier and the ball had also burst. The ball burst again during the 1947 FA Cup Final when the finalists again were Charlton Athletic, although this time their opponents were Burnley. Charlton won 1-0 in extra time.

ANOTHER FIRST AND TWO ONLYS IN THIS MATCH: The FIRST player to score for both sides in an FA Cup Final • The ONLY FA Cup victory for Derby County • The ONLY player to have won FA Cup winners' medals on either side of the Second World War – Raich Carter for Derby County, who also won a medal playing for Sunderland in 1937

THE FIRST
TEAM WITH COMMERCIAL SPONSORSHIP
Yeovil Town, 1948–1949

Shirt sponsorship, boot sponsorship, perimeter advertising and even stadium sponsorship (think Reebok Stadium, Emirates Stadium) is ubiquitous in modern football, but the first team sponsored by a commercial organization actually took to the field more than 60 years ago. For their FA Cup challenge in 1948–1949 Templeman's, a local shoe and boot company, sponsored non-League Yeovil Town's shirts and boots. The sponsorship obviously did them a power of good. Yeovil under Alec Stock, **the FIRST professional player-manager**, began their cup campaign with a 4-0 win at home to Romford on 27 November 1948 in the First Round. On 11 December they went away to Weymouth where they again won 4-0. On 8 January 1949 they beat Bury 3-1 in the Third Round and on 29 January 1949 in front of 16,318 fans – their record home attendance – they beat Sunderland (then sitting at eighth position in Division One) 2-1 in the Fourth Round. Their Cup odyssey came to an end on 12 February 1949 when they crashed out 8-0 to Manchester United before 81,565 fans at Maine Road.

THE FIRST
SCOTTISH TEAM TO
DO THE TREBLE
RANGERS, 1948–1949

For many years the big two – Celtic and Rangers – have dominated the Scottish league and cups. In 1949, under the managership of Bill Struth, Rangers became the first team to achieve the Treble – the League (by one point from Dundee), Scottish FA Cup (beating Clyde 4-1 in the Final on 23 April 1949) and Scottish League Cup (they defeated Raith Rovers 2-0 in the Final at Hampden Park on 12 March 1949). They repeated the feat in 1964, 1976, 1978, 1993, 1999 and 2003. Struth led Rangers to 18 League titles in his 34 years as manager before his health gave way and he retired in 1954. He died on 21 September 1956, aged 81.

THE FIRST
WORLD CUP MATCH FOR ENGLAND
ENGLAND V WALES AT NINIAN PARK, CARDIFF, GLAMORGAN, WALES, SATURDAY 15 OCTOBER 1949

The Home Championship doubled as a World Cup qualifying group and England got off to a good start in what was also their 250th official international. They beat Wales 4-1 and were four up at one stage. Newcastle United's Jackie Milburn scored a hat-trick.

THE FIRST
HOME WORLD CUP MATCH FOR ENGLAND
ENGLAND V IRELAND AT MAINE ROAD, MOSS SIDE, MANCHESTER, ENGLAND, WEDNESDAY 16 NOVEMBER 1949

England played their first home match in the World Cup (a Home Championship match as well) at Maine Road, Manchester and smashed

Ireland 9-2. Manchester United centre forward Jack Rowley hit four past Hugh Kelly in the Irish goal, while the other goals came from Portsmouth's Jack Froggatt making his international debut, two from Stan Pearson of Manchester United and two from Stan Mortensen of Blackpool.

THE ONLY
TEST CRICKETER WITH AN FA CUP WINNER'S MEDAL
Denis Compton, Arsenal v Liverpool at Wembley Stadium, Middlesex, England, Saturday 29 April 1950

Denis Compton, the first sportsman to advertise Brylcreem, spent the whole of his cricket career with Middlesex and the whole of his football career at Arsenal. He joined the MCC ground staff at Lord's in 1934. Four years later he scored his first Test century against Don Bradman's touring Australia. He played 78 Tests, scoring 5,807 runs with an average of 50.06 and hit 17 centuries with a highest score of 278. A winger, he made his debut for the Gunners in 1936, and won the League in 1948 and FA Cup in 1950. By the 1950 Final, when he appeared against Liverpool, he was already into his 30s, inclined to run out of puff and troubled by a notorious knee injury. In the first half, in his own words, he 'played a stinker'; in the second, fuelled by a mammoth slug of whisky administered by Alex James, he put in a dazzling performance.

THE ONLY
PLAYER WITH FA CUP LOSERS' MEDALS EITHER SIDE OF SECOND WORLD WAR
Willie Fagan, Preston North End v Sunderland at Wembley Stadium, Middlesex, England, Saturday 1 May 1937; Liverpool v Arsenal at Wembley Stadium, Middlesex, England, Saturday 29 April 1950

Born in Musselburgh, Scotland, Willie Fagan holds the record for being the only player on a losing FA Cup Final side both before and after the

Second World War. He was on the Preston North End side that lost to Sunderland in the first FA Cup Final broadcast and then joined Liverpool in October 1937. He returned to Anfield after the war, but found his appearances limited because of injury. He played 42 times in 1949–1950 including the FA Cup Final, but finished on the losing side again. He left Liverpool in January 1952 and later worked in a borstal. He died on Leap Year Day 1992.

THE FIRST
ENGLAND SUBSTITUTE
JIMMY MULLEN, ENGLAND V BELGIUM AT STADE DU HEYSEL, BRUSSELS, BELGIUM, THURSDAY 18 MAY 1950

In a friendly against Belgium watched by 55,854 spectators England manager Walter Winterbottom sent on the first international substitute as Jimmy Mullen replaced an injured Jackie Milburn after just 11 minutes. A minute after the second half began Mullen scored the first of England's four goals in the match.

THE FIRST
ENGLAND DEFEAT IN A WORLD CUP
ENGLAND V UNITED STATES OF AMERICA AT ESTÁDIO INDEPENDENCIA, BELO HORIZONTE, BRAZIL, 6 PM TUESDAY 29 JUNE 1950

In their first World Cup tournament England were drawn in Pool 2 along with Chile, Spain and the United States of America. They won their first match against Chile 2-0 and four days later went into the match complete favourites against the footballing minnows of America. The American team was made up of amateurs and semi-professionals, and they had spent the previous night trawling bars and most played the game with a hangover. Although England hit the post three times, it was a single goal,

JOE GAETJENS V PAPA DOC

Joseph Edouard Gaetjens was born at Port-au-Prince, Haiti on 19 March 1924 to a Haitian mother and a Belgian father. After studying accountancy at Columbia University, New York, he began playing semi-professional football in the American Soccer League. Despite playing for America he never became an American citizen. He customized his kit and despite pleas from his manager let his socks droop. After the World Cup he moved to France, before returning to Haiti in 1954 where he married and fathered three sons. He played for Haiti in a World Cup qualifier against Mexico on 27 December 1953. However, his family worked for a rival of Papa Doc Duvalier, Haiti's despotic leader, and his henchmen murdered Gaetjens's mother and elder brother while the rest of the family fled the country. Gaetjens, who ran a dry-cleaning business, refused to leave Haiti. On 8 July 1964 he was arrested by Papa Doc's secret police the Milice de Volontaires de la Sécurité Nationale, better known as the Tontons Macoutes, and taken to Fort Dimanche Prison. He was never seen again.

a diving header from Joe Gaetjens in the 37th minute, that sealed England's greatest footballing humiliation. Gaetjens later recalled, 'It was Walter Bahr that kicked it. All I did was dive.'

─••✦••─

THE ONLY
WORLD CUP NOT DECIDED BY A
ONE-MATCH FINAL
URUGUAY V BRAZIL AT ESTÁDIO DO MARACANÃ, RIO DE JANEIRO, BRAZIL, 3 PM FRIDAY 16 JULY 1950

Unlike every other World Cup, the 1950 tournament – the first for 12 years – was decided on a group contest between Brazil, Spain, Sweden and Uruguay. The competition was in the end settled by the final match, with Brazil needing just a draw to win the Jules Rimet Trophy. Inside right Friaça scored in the 47th minute to give Brazil the lead, but on the 66th minute Juan Alberto Schiaffino equalized for Uruguay. With 11 minutes remaining on the clock inside right Alcides Ghiggia hit the winning goal to give the World Cup to Uruguay for the second time in their history. The referee was George Reader, **the FIRST Englishman to take charge of (what turned out to be) a World Cup Final**.

THE LAST
AMATEUR PLAYER
IN AN FA CUP FINAL
BILL SLATER, BLACKPOOL V NEWCASTLE AT WEMBLEY STADIUM, MIDDLESEX, ENGLAND, SATURDAY 28 APRIL 1951

Inside left Bill Slater became the last amateur to play for a professional team in an FA Cup Final when he appeared on the losing Blackpool side as the Magpies won 2-0. Born in 1927, he joined Blackpool in 1944 as an amateur and maintained his status, making his first team debut in 1949. He played 30 times for Blackpool before moving to Brentford in December 1951. In August 1952 he signed for Wolverhampton Wanderers as a part-time professional. He stayed at Molineux until 1963, making more than 300 appearances. He became captain and having changed his playing position to centre back led them to their victorious 1960 FA Cup win against Blackburn Rovers.

THE FIRST
SCOTLAND
PLAYER SENT OFF
BILLY STEEL, SCOTLAND V AUSTRIA AT PRATER STADIUM, VIENNA, AUSTRIA, 3 PM SUNDAY 27 MAY 1951

Billy Steel of Dundee was the first player to be sent off while on international duty for Scotland in a match that ended in a 4-0 defeat. It was his 12th cap and Scotland's 217th game. Steel joined Dundee in 1950 for a fee of £17,500, and in four years at Dens Park won two League Cup medals in 1952 and 1953 and played in the Scottish Cup Final of 1952. In 1954 he moved to the USA to play for the Los Angeles Danes. He died on 13 May 1982.

THE ONLY
MAN TO PLAY
WORLD CUP FOOTBALL AND TEST CRICKET
FOR ENGLAND

WILLIE WATSON, ENGLAND V IRELAND AT MAINE ROAD, MOSS SIDE, MANCHESTER, ENGLAND, WEDNESDAY 16 NOVEMBER 1949; ENGLAND V SOUTH AFRICA AT TRENT BRIDGE, NOTTINGHAM, ENGLAND, THURSDAY 7 JUNE 1951

Born on 7 March 1920 in Bolton on Dearne, Yorkshire, Willie Watson is the only man to have played in a World Cup match for England and also Test cricket for England. A left-handed batsman, he made his debut for Yorkshire on 22 July 1939 against Nottinghamshire at Bramall Lane, Sheffield, only to have his career interrupted by the Second World War. He resumed his career when peace was proclaimed and made 223 League appearances for Sunderland in seven seasons at Roker Park. He made his international football debut (one of four appearances for his country) in the first World Cup-qualifying home match played by England, a 9-2 victory over Ireland at Maine Road. However, he did not appear in any matches played during the final stages of the World Cup in Brazil in 1950.

The following year in June 1951 he made his Test debut against South Africa, the first of 23 appearances. He scored 109 over almost six hours in the second Test in 1953 at Lord's against the Australians when the match appeared all but lost. He was not picked for The Oval Test when the Ashes were regained after 19 years. In 1954 he was named as one of *Wisden's* five Cricketers of the Year. That year he became manager of Halifax Town, a position he held until 1956. In 1958 he left his native county and joined Leicestershire CCC as assistant secretary and captain. He retired in 1962, although he made nine appearances in 1963 and 1964.

That was the year he undertook a second spell as manager at Shay Ground, which lasted two years. From 1966 until 1968 he was manager of Bradford City. He died on 23 April 2004.

THE FIRST
WHITE FOOTBALLS
1951

In 1951 the Football League introduced white footballs to the English game, but despite their higher visibility, it was not until 1954 that the white ball became a regular sight on the English pitch. The change came because of a televised match between Wolverhampton Wanderers and Honvéd from Hungary on 13 December 1954 when Wolves won 3-2. The visitor's side featured six of the players who had beaten England 6-3 at Wembley in November 1953. The BBC broadcast the second half of the match, which allowed viewers to see the visual superiority of the white ball, and not long after many clubs began to use it. The year 1954 also saw the first 32-panelled balls, which were made in Denmark. It would not be until the 1960s that an all-synthetic ball would be used.

THE FIRST
WINNERS OF SUCCESSIVE FA CUP FINALS IN THE 20TH CENTURY
Newcastle United v Blackpool at Wembley Stadium, Middlesex, England, Saturday 28 April 1951; Newcastle United v Arsenal at Wembley Stadium, Middlesex, England, Saturday 3 May 1952

In 1952 Newcastle United became the first team to win successive FA Cup Finals in the 20th century. They beat Blackpool in 1951 and then saw off the challenge of Arsenal who had won the trophy in 1950 beating

Liverpool. That year Arsenal were on the other side of the famous result as Newcastle won 1-0. The Arsenal team was beset with injuries both before and during the game. Ray Daniel played with a broken wrist, Doug Lishman had a septic wound and Jimmy Logie had internal bleeding from a leg wound. Wally Barnes injured himself after 35 minutes and had to go off for treatment. He hobbled back on, but the pain was too much and Arsenal were reduced to ten men for the rest of the Final. With six minutes to go Holton and Roper were injured, but referee Arthur Ellis waved play on and Bobby Mitchell crossed for George Robledo to head home Newcastle's winner.

ANOTHER FIRST IN THIS MATCH:

The **FIRST** man to win the FA Cup as player and manager – **Stan Seymour** of Newcastle United, having previously netted a goal for Newcastle when they beat Aston Villa in the Final on 27 April 1924

———— ◆ ————

THE LAST

PLAYER TO DATE TO SCORE A HAT-TRICK IN AN FA CUP FINAL

STAN MORTENSEN, BLACKPOOL V BOLTON WANDERERS AT WEMBLEY STADIUM, MIDDLESEX, ENGLAND, SATURDAY 2 MAY 1953

The eighth post-war Wembley Cup Final was fought between two northern teams. Stan Mortensen became the third and, to date, last player to score an FA Cup Final hat-trick when he put three past Bolton in 1953. Wanderers scored the highest number of goals for a losing team in the match. The Bolton players were paid £20 and given a commemorative cigarette lighter by the grateful club. Despite Mortensen's three goals, the Final is known to history as the Matthews Final because teammate Stanley Matthews inspired his team to victory after being 3-1 down.

THE FIRST

ABANDONED ENGLAND MATCH

**ENGLAND V ARGENTINA AT EL MONUMENAL, BUENOS AIRES,
ARGENTINA, SUNDAY 17 MAY 1953**

In pouring rain and with a waterlogged pitch England took to the field in South America. As captain Billy Wright went for the toss-up, Nat Lofthouse joked, 'If you win Billy, attack the deep end.' The match lasted just 23 minutes before English referee Arthur Ellis suspended the game. After 36 minutes when conditions had not improved he called an end to proceedings telling the press, 'If we had stayed out any longer we would have needed lifeboats.' Only two other England games have been abandoned – one through fog (29 October 1975 against Czechoslovakia in Bratislava) and the other because of crowd trouble (against Ireland in Dublin on 15 March 1995).

THE FIRST

ENGLAND INTERNATIONAL DEFEAT
IN ENGLAND

ENGLAND V HUNGARY AT WEMBLEY STADIUM, MIDDLESEX, ENGLAND,
WEDNESDAY 25 NOVEMBER 1953

The supposedly invincible England team lined up against a Hungarian side that included the likes of Ferenc Puskás and Sándor Kocsis before 100,000 spectators. Still, the press gave the foreigners no chance and everyone confidently expected an England win. Captain Billy Wright later commented:

'*We completely underestimated the advances that Hungary had made, and not only tactically. When we walked out at Wembley that afternoon, side by side with the visiting team, I looked down and noticed that the Hungarians had on these strange, lightweight boots, cut away like slippers under the ankle bone. I turned to big Stan Mortensen and said, "We should be all right here, Stan, they haven't got the proper kit."*'

The Magyars gave England a lesson in the beautiful game and Nándor Hidegkuti put them one up after just 90 seconds. Jackie Sewell of Sheffield Wednesday pulled it back to one-all after 13 minutes, but Hidegkuti made it 2-1 to the visitors 13 minutes later. Ferenc Puskás scored on 24 and 27 minutes to make it 4-1 at half-time. Stan Mortensen of Blackpool made it 2-4, but the Hungarians were not to be stopped. József Bozsik made it 5-2 on 50 minutes and Hidegkuti made it 6 three minutes later with his hat-trick. Alf Ramsey of Spurs managed a consolatory third for England in the 57th minute, but the myth of England invincibility had been well and truly crushed. On 23 May 1954 a return game was organized in Budapest and Sir Stanley Rous, the secretary of the Football Association, told the press that there would be no repeat of the Wembley embarrassment: 'I assure you, gentlemen, the result last November was an aberration. This time England will win.' Rous was partly right – there was no repeat of the Wembley embarrassment. This time it was a fiasco – Hungary 7 England 1.

THE ONLY
WORLD CUP MATCH DECIDED BY A
BLINDFOLDED BOY
SPAIN V TURKEY AT ROME, ITALY, WEDNESDAY 17 MARCH 1954

For some reason, when Fifa arranged the 13 qualifying groups for the 1954 World Cup they didn't divide them equally. Most groups had three countries participating, while some had just two. The only group with four countries was Group 3 and that was because it was the Home Championship. (There were four countries in Group 11, but Peru withdrew before the competition started.) Group 5 contained just Austria and Portugal, with Austria winning the first match 9-1 and drawing 0-0 in the second. Group 7 was Hungary and Poland and the Poles withdrew before the first match. Group 9 was just Egypt and Italy. There were only two in Group 13 after Taiwan withdrew.

There were also only two teams in Group 6 for the 1954 World Cup Finals in Switzerland – Spain and Turkey. Both teams fancied their chances before the matches, but that view changed when Spain won the game in Madrid convincingly by four goals to one on 6 January 1954. The return match was not a goalfest, Turkey winning 1-0 on 14 March 1954. Now most neutrals would believe that Spain should qualify for Basle, winning 4-2 on aggregate. That was not Fifa's thinking, however. Both teams had won one match, were therefore equal and must play a decider in neutral Rome. The game ended 2-2 after extra time, so rather than find a sporting way of deciding a winner, Fifa asked 14-year-old Italian Luigi Franco Gemma to draw straws to find the winner. To ensure that he didn't cheat, Fifa officials blindfolded the boy. Thus it was that Turkey went to the World Cup in Switzerland and Spain didn't.

THE ONLY
PLAYER TO WIN
SCOTTISH FA CUP, THE FA CUP AND
NORTHERN IRISH CUP MEDALS

JIMMY DELANEY, CELTIC V ABERDEEN AT HAMPDEN PARK, MOUNT FLORIDA, GLASGOW, LANARKSHIRE, SCOTLAND, SATURDAY 24 APRIL 1937; MANCHESTER UNITED V BLACKPOOL AT WEMBLEY STADIUM, MIDDLESEX, ENGLAND, SATURDAY 24 APRIL 1948; DERRY CITY V GLENTORAN AT WINDSOR PARK, DONEGALL AVENUE, BELFAST, COUNTY ANTRIM, NORTHERN IRELAND, MONDAY 10 MAY 1954

Scottish international winger Jimmy Delaney completed a unique treble in 1954. He won a Cup winner's medal with Derry City in Ireland when they beat Glentoran 1-0 in a replay. Six years earlier he had won an FA Cup medal with Manchester United when they beat Blackpool 4-2 at Wembley and 11 years before that he had picked up a Scottish Cup medal with Celtic when they beat Aberdeen 2-1. He very nearly made it four medals in four Cup competitions, but had to settle for a runners-up gong with Cork City against Shamrock Rovers in the FAI Cup in 1956. He died in 1989.

THE FIRST

GERMAN TO PLAY IN AN FA CUP FINAL

Bert Trautmann, Manchester City v Newcastle United at Wembley
Stadium, Middlesex, England, Saturday 7 May 1955

Bert Trautmann was a former Second World War German paratrooper
who won the Iron Cross before he was captured and imprisoned in
Ashton-in-Makerfield, Lancashire. Trautmann was released at the end of
the war, but decided to stay in England and began work on a farm,
spending his spare time keeping goal for local side St Helens Town. In
October 1949 he signed for Manchester City, but at first there was
opposition to having a decorated former German soldier playing for an
English Division One team. Trautmann's skill won the fans over and he
went on to play for City until 1964, making 508 appearances.

In 1955 he became the first German to play in an FA Cup Final when
Manchester City met Newcastle. For the superstitious among the players
and fans, Newcastle had the same dressing room as when they met (and
beat) Arsenal in 1952. The Geordies went into the lead after just 45 seconds
when Jackie Milburn headed the ball into Trautmann's goal from a Len
White corner. On 22 minutes City right back Jimmy Meadows was injured
trying to stop Bobby Mitchell and played no further part in the game (again,
the superstitious would have noted that Arsenal lost Wally Barnes in 1952
after he tried to tackle Mitchell in the same corner). City equalized in the
44th minute through a diving header from Bobby Johnstone, one of two
Scots in the team. The extra man began to tell for Newcastle in the second
half and despite Trautmann's best efforts the Geordies ran out 3-1 winners.

THE FIRST

FOOTBALL LEAGUE MATCH
PLAYED UNDER FLOODLIGHTS

PORTSMOUTH V NEWCASTLE UNITED AT FRATTON PARK, FROGMORE ROAD, PORTSMOUTH,
HAMPSHIRE, ENGLAND, WEDNESDAY 22 FEBRUARY 1956

In 1930 Arsenal's visionary manager Herbert Chapman paid a visit to
Belgium and watched a game under floodlights. He immediately saw a

potential new way to expand the game. Chapman arranged for lights to be installed at Highbury both for the main pitch and the practice one. However, the footballing authorities refused to let them be used for League matches. It would not be until 1951 that a game was first played under floodlights at Highbury. **The FIRST FA Cup match under floodlights** was on 28 November 1955 for a First Round replay between Carlisle United and Darlington at St James' Park, Newcastle, when Darlington won 3-1. It was 1956 before lights became a fixture at football grounds and the first floodlit Football League match took place at Fratton Park, Portsmouth between Portsmouth and Newcastle United. The game was held up for 30 minutes when the fuses failed. **The FIRST floodlit League match in Scotland** was on 7 March 1956 at Ibrox, when Rangers beat Queen of the South 8-0. (See 1878, page 30.)

(See 1878, page 30.)

THE FIRST

PLAYER TO SCORE IN CONSECUTIVE WEMBLEY FINALS

Bobby Johnstone, Manchester City v Birmingham City at Wembley Stadium, Middlesex, England, 3 pm Saturday 5 May 1956

Having become the first German to play in the FA Cup Final the previous year, Manchester City returned almost a year to the day to give Bert Trautmann, their Iron Cross-winning goalie, another shot at a winner's medal. To accommodate both teams hailing from north of Watford, British Railways laid on 38 special trains, the first arriving at St Pancras from Manchester shortly after 3 am, almost 12 hours before kick-off. Programme sellers were also out early to prevent unofficial vendors making money. As in 1931 the *Birmingham Mail* produced a special edition of their Saturday sports paper *Sports Argus* on blue paper rather than the usual pink. As the teams left the tunnel, Manchester City captain Roy Paul stopped, raised his fist and shouted at his team, 'If we don't f***** win, you'll get some of this.' Both teams changed their strip: Birmingham City took to the field in white shirts with black trim, black shorts and black stockings with white tops, while their Manchester rivals wore maroon and white striped shirts, white shorts and maroon stockings with three white hoops at the top.

Birmingham won the toss and kicked off, but it was Manchester City who took the lead after just three minutes through inside right Joe Hayes. Noel Kinsey, Birmingham City's inside right, levelled the scores on 15 minutes and that's the way the score stayed at half-time, although the team from St Andrew's had two goals disallowed because Eddy Brown was offside.

There were fiery arguments in both dressing rooms over the break and both teams came out raring to get stuck in. On 62 minutes Bobby Johnstone put Manchester City into the lead, becoming the first player to score in consecutive Wembley finals. Two minutes later inside left Jack Dyson made it 3-1. In the 73rd minute Trautmann came out to dive at the feet of Birmingham City's Peter Murphy and as he did so Murphy's knee hit him in the neck, knocking Trautmann unconscious. Referee Alf Bond stopped play and trainer Laurie Barnett ran onto the pitch with his magic sponge. Barnett worked on the stricken goalie for some time, and although no one realized it at the time, in making the save Trautmann had broken his neck. Manchester City captain Roy Paul thought that the team would be better served by putting Roy Little between the sticks, but Trautmann insisted on carrying on despite being in tremendous pain. The Manchester players rallied round the keeper, kicking the ball away from the goal as often as they could, but Trautmann still had to make two saves, one of which required Laurie Barnett to revive him.

Many commented that the goalie's neck looked crooked as he collected his winner's medal, including the Duke of Edinburgh. Three days after the Final, an X-ray at the Manchester Royal Infirmary revealed the awful truth. That year Trautmann became **the FIRST continental-born player named Footballer of the Year**.

BERT TRAUTMANN WAS ALSO: The ONLY goalkeeper to play in an FA Cup Final with a broken neck

THE ONLY

FOUR-WAY TIE
IN THE HOME CHAMPIONSHIP

1955–1956

Beginning in 1883–1884, there was only one occasion when all four competing nations – England, Northern Ireland, Scotland and Wales – tied for the title of Home Champions. In the 73rd Home Championship each team won one, drew one and lost one, finishing on three points. Had goal difference been used to separate the teams, England would have won with Scotland second, Wales third and Northern Ireland being awarded the wooden spoon.

THE FIRST

ENGLISH TEAM TO COMPETE IN EUROPE

BIRMINGHAM CITY V INTER MILAN IN INTER-CITIES FAIRS CUP AT SAN SIRO, MILAN, ITALY, TUESDAY 15 MAY 1956

Birmingham City became the first English team to compete in Europe when they travelled to Milan to play Inter Milan in the first Inter-Cities Fairs Cup competition. The tournament – the forerunner to the Uefa Cup – featured cities rather than teams (they had to have staged a trade fair since the Second World War) and was played over three seasons. Birmingham City were drawn in Group B with Inter Milan and a Zagreb XI. In Group D were a London XI (managed by Chelsea chairman Joe Mears), a Basle XI and a Frankfurt XI. The Blues won three of their four games, conceding just one goal (ironically against Inter Milan), drawing the opening match 0-0 with Inter Milan and progressing to the Semi-Final, where they lost a replay to Barcelona after an aggregate score of 4-4. London XI got through to the Final, where they lost 8-2 to Barcelona on aggregate (2-2, 0-6). Jimmy Greaves was **the FIRST English player to score in a major European final** – he got London XI's opener in the First Leg.

THE FIRST

EUROPEAN
CUP FINAL

REAL MADRID V STADE DE REIMS-CHAMPAGNE AT PARC DES PRINCES,
PARIS, FRANCE, WEDNESDAY 13 JUNE 1956

The idea of a pan-European champions' cup was mooted in 1926, but it took almost 30 years for it to finally get off the ground when Uefa agreed to the European Cup on 8 May 1955. English champions Chelsea and Hibernian from Scotland were the first British representatives. Hibernian were not the previous season's champions – Aberdeen were – but Uefa thought that their recent record was better than Aberdeen's. In the First Round Chelsea were drawn against the Swedish side Djurgården, but had to pull out on the orders of the Football Association and the Football League, leaving Hibs to fly the flag alone for Britain. Sixteen teams contested the first European Cup and the Final was fought between a Spanish team and one from France in front of 38,000 spectators. Real Madrid reached the final in Paris by beating AC Milan 5-4 on aggregate in the Semi-Finals, while their French opponents beat Hibernian 3-0 on aggregate. After six minutes Stade de Reims-Champagne scored through centre half Michel Leblond and forward Jean Templin added a second four

RULE BRITANNIA

All the officials in the match hailed from England. The referee was Arthur Ellis who had been in the middle in the 1950, 1954 and 1958 World Cups. He would later become a member of the first Pools Panel in 1963 and the man with the dipstick as the final arbiter on *It's a Knockout*. He died of prostate cancer on 23 May 1999 at the age of 84. One of the linesmen in Paris was called Tommy Cooper.

minutes later. Alfredo di Stéfano pulled one back on the 14th minute and Héctor Rial equalized on the half-hour mark, and that was the way it stayed at half-time. On 62 minutes Michel Hidalgo put the Frenchmen into the lead again, only for left back Marquitos to again level the scores in the 67th minute, and 12 minutes later Rial scored his second and Real's fourth to win the match for the Spaniards. It would be the first of five consecutive European Cup wins for Real Madrid.

——••—•—••——

THE LAST
MATCH PLAYED IN ENGLAND
BY THE BUSBY BABES

ARSENAL V MANCHESTER UNITED AT ARSENAL STADIUM, AVENELL ROAD, HIGHBURY, LONDON, ENGLAND, SATURDAY 1 FEBRUARY 1958

The youthful team assembled by Matt Busby at Old Trafford was expected to sweep all comers before them for many years, but fate was to intervene. The last match played in England by the Busby Babes before their journey to Belgrade was at Arsenal Stadium. The game was played before 63,578 spectators and was thrilling end-to-end stuff. After ten minutes Duncan Edwards put United one in front, Jack Kelsey not having a chance to block the powerful shot. Bobby Charlton put the northerners two up after half an hour. Tommy Taylor made it 3-0 and that was the way the score stayed until the second half. As with future and past teams, Arsenal refused to lie down and die and David Herd pulled one back before Jimmy Bloomfield scored twice to bring the score to three-all. Dennis Viollet headed home for 4-3 to United. Taylor scored in the second half to make it 5-3. Derek Tapscott scored what would be his last goal for Arsenal to take the score to 5-4 – he moved to Division Two Cardiff City in September of 1958 for £10,000. It ended that way, although Vic Groves almost equalized. Tapscott later commented, 'I were the last fella to score against the Busby Babes in England. But I wish to God I wasn't.' (See 1958, page 108.)

THE LAST

MATCH PLAYED BY THE BUSBY BABES

RED STAR BELGRADE V MANCHESTER UNITED AT STADION JNA, BELGRADE, YUGOSLAVIA, WEDNESDAY 5 FEBRUARY 1958

On 14 January 1958 Manchester United had beaten Red Star Belgrade 2-1 at Old Trafford. United chartered a plane to take them to the Second Leg, which they drew 3-3 (Bobby Charlton getting two and Dennis Viollet one), although they led 3-0 at one stage. The British European Airways Flight 609 was delayed leaving Zemun Airport, Belgrade for an hour because United outside right Johnny Berry had lost his passport. The plane didn't have a sufficient range to travel directly to Manchester and so made a stop at Munich in West Germany to refuel, landing at 1.15 pm. After the plane received new supplies, an attempt to take off was made and abandoned because the pilot thought the engine sounded odd. A second attempt was also abandoned and the players were told to disembark.

With a light snow now falling much more heavily, it looked as if the passengers would have to spend the night in Munich. Indeed, Duncan Edwards sent a telegram to his landlady saying that he would not be home until the next day: 'All flights cancelled. Flying tomorrow. Duncan.' However, after 15 minutes the passengers were recalled to the plane. By this time the runway at Munich-Riem Airport was covered in slush. At 3.03 pm the pilots Captain James Thain and Captain Kenneth Rayment attempted a third take-off. Some of the United players had been part of a card school and before the third attempt they all moved to the back of the plane apart from Albert Scanlon. (He was the only one of the school to survive, albeit with terrible injuries; he left United in 1960, disappointed by the way he believed the club had treated him, and died on 22 December 2009.) The plane did not achieve sufficient speed to take off and skidded off the runway, crashing through a fence and into a house, a tree and a wooden hut.

Out of 44 people on board, 23 including eight of the United squad (full back Geoff Bent, 25; full back and club captain Roger Byrne, two days before his 29th birthday; wing half Eddie Colman, 21, the youngest to die;

wing half Duncan Edwards in hospital on 21 February 1958, aged 21; centre half Mark Jones, 24; left winger David Pegg, 22; centre forward Tommy Taylor, 26; and inside forward Billy Whelan, 22) perished as a result of the crash. Nine players survived, but two of them, Johnny Berry (died 16 September 1994) and Jackie Blanchflower (died 2 September 1998), brother of Tottenham Hotspur's Danny, never played again. United secretary Walter Crickmer also died, along with the 63-year-old first team trainer Tom Curry and coach Bert Whalley, 45. Matt Busby suffered extensive injuries and was the only club official to survive the crash. Eight of the nine journalists on board also died: Alf Clarke (*Manchester Evening Chronicle*); Donny Davies (*Manchester Guardian*), 65, who had also been a First Class cricketer for Lancashire; George Follows (*Daily Herald*); Tom Jackson (*Manchester Evening News*); Archie Ledbrooke (*Daily Mirror*); Henry Rose (*Daily Express*); Eric Thompson (*Daily Mail*) and on the way to hospital Frank Swift (*News of the World*), aged 44. The programme for United's next home match (against Sheffield Wednesday on 19 February 1958 in the Fifth Round of the FA Cup) contained no players' names, just 11 blank spaces.

The cause of the crash was the build-up of slush on the runway, although the West German authorities blamed Captain Thain (Captain Rayment died of brain damage three weeks after the crash) and he was not absolved until 1969. He died on 6 August 1975, aged 54, of a heart attack, a broken man. Documents declassified in 2007 showed that, while the English authorities privately took Captain Thain's side all along, they did not exert more public pressure to avoid embarrassing the West Germans in the fraught post-war atmosphere. Harry Gregg, the United goalkeeper and one of the survivors, later said of the pilot, 'Jim Thain was a good man and was crucified.'

TOO LITTLE TOO LATE?

Many of the survivors of Munich and their families believed that Manchester United didn't do enough to help them financially. The club didn't organize a testimonial until 40 years had passed.

THE ONLY
LEAGUE CLUB TO
SCORE AND CONCEDE
100 GOALS IN A SEASON
MANCHESTER CITY, 1957–1958

In the season that saw tragedy befall their Manchester neighbours, the Sky Blues of Maine Road scored an incredible 104 goals in Division One. The attack may have been on form, but the defence was lamentable – Manchester City conceded 100 goals. They finished in fifth position, 15 points behind champions Wolverhampton Wanderers. (See 1937–1938, page 83.)

THE ONLY
'CUP-TIED'
FA CUP FINALIST
Stan Crowther, Manchester United v Bolton Wanderers at Wembley
Stadium, Middlesex, England, 3 pm Saturday 3 May 1958

It is usual practice that if a player appears for one team in an FA Cup (or any cup) tie and then is transferred, he cannot appear for his new club in the same competition. The Football Association gave a special dispensation to Stan Crowther in 1958. He had played for Aston Villa in the early stages of the Cup and then signed for Manchester United for £18,000, as caretaker boss Jimmy Murphy desperately tried to replace those players killed at Munich. Crowther was allowed to play in the Final, which United lost 2-0 to Bolton. United had got to the Final by beating Fulham 5-3 after a replay and Alex Dawson became **the LAST player to date to score a hat-trick in an FA Cup Semi-Final**. Crowther did not fit in at Old Trafford and left after playing just 20 games.

THE ONLY

PLAYER UNABLE TO PLAY IN THE WORLD CUP BECAUSE HE WAS SENT TO SIBERIA

EDUARD STRELTSOV, UNION OF SOVIET SOCIALIST REPUBLICS, 1958

The name of Eduard Streltsov is now little known, but in the 1950s he was the leading footballer in the Communist world. Born in 1937, he was outstanding in the 1956 Olympic Games. It is believed that had he been able to go to Sweden he would have set the world stage alight, perhaps even outshining Pelé. On 25 May 1958 he left the USSR's pre-World Cup training camp at Tarasovka just outside Moscow and attended a party at a dacha owned by military officer Eduard Karakhanov. Sometime during the party Streltsov, who had married a year before, allegedly raped 20-year-old Marina Lebedeva. Arrested the next morning, he was told that if he pleaded guilty he would be allowed to play in the World Cup, only to be sentenced to 12 years in a Siberian gulag when he did.

Some believe that Streltsov was set up by Yekaterina Furtseva, the only woman to become a member of the Politburo, after he insulted her 16-year-old daughter, Svetlana, at a Kremlin ball. However, there is an alternative theory that the arrogant player was indeed guilty. Few of his surviving teammates were prepared to defend him when questioned more than 40 years after the event. Photographs – perhaps doctored – exist of an assaulted Lebedeva and Streltsov with scratches on his face. Soviet justice didn't usually need such damning evidence.

Streltsov was attacked in the camp and spent four months in the prison hospital recuperating. He was released and in 1963 resumed his football career with Torpedo – the smallest of the five Moscow sides. In his first season back he led them to the league title. In 1967 and 1968 he was named Soviet Player of the Year. Yekaterina Furtseva committed suicide on 24 October 1974. Lebedeva has vanished. Streltsov died of throat cancer in 1990.

THE FIRST

EUROPEAN
CUP FINAL TO GO TO
EXTRA TIME

**Real Madrid v AC Milan at Stade du Heysel, Brussels, Belgium,
Wednesday 28 May 1958**

The third European Cup Final was the first that needed another 30 minutes to decide the result. At 90 minutes the score was 2-2 with Alfredo di Stéfano and Héctor Rial scoring for Real, and Schiaffino and Grillo hitting the back of the net for AC Milan. Franciso Gento added a third in extra time to give the Cup to Real for the third consecutive year. There were 37,290 spectators inside the Heysel Stadium for the match.

THE ONLY

WORLD CUP FINALS AT WHICH
ALL FOUR HOME NATIONS QUALIFIED

SWEDEN, 1958

The sixth World Cup was the only one in which England, Northern Ireland, Scotland and Wales all qualified for the finals. England topped a group that included Ireland and Denmark, and Scotland and Northern Ireland also finished at the head of their respective groups. Wales made it to Scandinavia after beating Israel in a play-off following the withdrawal of East Germany. On the way to Sweden Jackie Mudie became **the FIRST Scotsman to score a World Cup hat-trick** when he hit three against Spain on 8 May 1957 as Scotland won 4-2.

THE FIRST
ENGLISH WORLD CUP FINAL
MANAGER

GEORGE RAYNOR, SWEDEN V BRAZIL AT RAASUNDA STADIUM, SOLNA,
SWEDEN, SUNDAY 29 JUNE 1958

George Raynor was the first Englishman to manage a side that reached the World Cup Final when he led Sweden almost to glory in 1958. They lost the final 5-2 to Brazil. Born at Wombwell, Yorkshire on 13 January 1907, he played non-League football before joining Sheffield United in 1930, but made just one League appearance in two years before beginning a peripatetic existence until the Second World War. After cessation of hostilities he was appointed manager of Sweden. He led them to Olympic gold in 1948, beating Yugoslavia 3-1 in the final. Two years later Sweden finished in third place in the World Cup. A bronze medal followed at the 1952 Olympic Games in Helsinki. Sweden were runners-up to Brazil in the 1954 World Cup and five years later Sweden became only the second foreign side to beat England at Wembley. He also found time to manage club sides including AIK Stockholm, Lazio and Skegness Town. He died on 24 November 1985.

THE ONLY
PLAYER TO HAVE REPRESENTED ENGLAND
AND PLAYED FOR HIS CLUB
ON SAME DAY

DANNY CLAPTON, ENGLAND V WALES AT VILLA PARK,
TRINITY ROAD, BIRMINGHAM, ENGLAND; ARSENAL V JUVENTUS
AT ARSENAL STADIUM, AVENELL ROAD, HIGHBURY, LONDON,
ENGLAND, WEDNESDAY 26 NOVEMBER 1958

On a cold afternoon in 1958 Danny Clapton made his debut for England against Wales at the home of Aston Villa in a match that England drew

2-2. In goal for Wales that day was Arsenal's Jack Kelsey and watching in the stands was Tommy Docherty, there on behalf of Scotland's caretaker manager Matt Busby. It would be Clapton's only international appearance. When the match was over Clapton and Kelsey piled into Docherty's car and they drove to Highbury, where all three turned out for Arsenal in a friendly against Juventus. The Gunners won 3-1 with goals from John Barnwell, Roy Goulden and Jimmy Bloomfield before 51,107 fans.

IN THE SAME WAY, JACK KELSEY WAS:
The ONLY player to have represented Wales and played for his club on the same day

THE FIRST
PLAYER TO WIN
100 ENGLAND CAPS
BILLY WRIGHT, ENGLAND V SCOTLAND AT WEMBLEY STADIUM, MIDDLESEX, ENGLAND, SATURDAY 11 APRIL 1959

Billy Wright won his first cap for England against Ireland at Windsor Park on 28 September 1946 as England won 7-2. A centre half, he captained his country on a remarkable 90 occasions of his 105 appearances (Bobby Moore was to later equal the record). Wright was the world's first player to win 100 caps for his country and Wright's 100th came during the Home Championship match against Scotland when Bobby Charlton scored the only goal with a header in the second half. Ironically, it would be Charlton who broke Wright's record for the most England caps. Wright turned out professionally for only one club in his career, Wolverhampton Wanderers, and under his captaincy they won the FA Cup in 1949 and the League Championship in 1954, 1958 and 1959.

THE FIRST

ENGLAND TEAM PICKED BY THE MANAGER

ENGLAND V SWEDEN AT WEMBLEY STADIUM, MIDDLESEX, ENGLAND, WEDNESDAY 28 OCTOBER 1959

Despite being appointed England director of coaching on 28 September 1946 (and manager in May 1947), Walter Winterbottom had never had the sole responsibility of choosing the side that represented England. He was merely an adviser to a Football Association committee. Finally, he managed to let the committee allow him to pick the team for the match against Sweden. He told the FA's wise men that he wanted to build a team capable of winning the World Cup, so they let him have his way. The team Winterbottom picked was: 1 Eddie Hopkinson (Bolton Wanderers, winning his 14th and last cap), 2 Don Howe (West Bromwich Albion, winning his 22nd out of 23 caps), 3 Tony Allen (Stoke City, winning his second of three caps), 4 captain Ronnie Clayton (Blackburn Rovers, his 32nd out of 35 caps), 5 Trevor Smith (Birmingham City, his second and final appearance in an England shirt), 6 Ron Flowers (Wolverhampton Wanderers, winning his 10th of 49 caps), 7 John Connelly (Burnley, his second of what would be 20 caps), 8 Jimmy Greaves (Chelsea, winning his fifth of 57 caps), 9 Brian Clough (Middlesbrough, winning his second and last cap), 10 Bobby Charlton (Manchester United, his 14th of 106 caps) and 11 Edwin Holliday (Middlesbrough, winning his second of three caps). Among the reserves were Ron Springett and George Eastham.

In front of 72,000 spectators England lost 3-2 – their second defeat against foreigners on home soil – after which the FA took away Winterbottom's prerogative and went back to selection by committee. Seven years later Springett, Flowers, Connelly, Greaves, Eastham and Charlton were part of the squad that won the World Cup for England under Alf Ramsey.

THE FIRST
PLAYER AT A SCOTTISH CLUB
TO REPRESENT ENGLAND

Joe Baker of Hibernian, England v Northern Ireland at Wembley
Stadium, Middlesex, England, Wednesday 18 November 1959

Playing outside of your home country tended to prevent selection for the
national side, but in 1959 England manager Walter Winterbottom chose
Liverpool-born centre forward Joe Baker (1940–2003) of Hibernian to
make his debut in the match against Northern Ireland in the Home
Championships. Baker was the first player to represent England despite
never having played in England. (Owen Hargreaves is only the second
player in the same position.) The gamble paid off as Baker scored and
England won 2-1. Two years later he signed for Torino and then in July
1962 spent four successful years at Arsenal where he scored 100 goals in
156 appearances. At 5 ft 7 in (1.70 m) he was on the short side for a striker,
but this did not stop him hitting the back of the net more than 300 times.
Baker died aged 63 on 6 October 2003 of a heart attack while playing golf.

THE ONLY
BRITISH FOOTBALLER
TO WIN AN OSCAR

Neil Paterson, RKO Pantages Theatre, Los Angeles, California,
United States of America, Monday 4 April 1960

James Edmund Neil Paterson was born at Greenock, Renfrewshire on New
Year's Eve 1915, the son of a lawyer. After Edinburgh University he
became a sub-editor on women's magazines for DC Thomson-Leng
Publications in Dundee and wrote romantic stories. After playing football
for Buckie Thistle and Leith Athletic he joined Dundee United as an
amateur and in 1936 he became captain. He had little interest in football
other than as a hobby and left to return to journalism. After the Second

World War he began winning awards for his writing. In 1948 he wrote the novel *The China Run: The Biography of a Great-Grandmother*, which was selected as book of the year by Somerset Maugham in the *New York Times*. In 1950 he published *Behold Thy Daughter*, becoming a bestseller in a dozen languages. A short story he wrote entitled *Scotch Settlement* was turned into a film called *The Kidnappers* (1953). That year he also wrote *Man on the Tightrope*, a political thriller, after which he wrote screenplays. He won an Oscar for Best Writing, Screenplay Based on Material from Another Medium for his adaptation of John Braine's novel about ambitious young accountant Joe Lampton (Laurence Harvey), *Room at the Top* (released January 1959). Not long afterwards Paterson retired and spent his time playing golf, salmon fishing and sitting on the directorial boards of various institutions. He died at Crieff on 19 April 1995, aged 79.

THE FIRST
EUROPEAN CHAMPIONSHIP
1960

Originally called the European Nations Cup, the competition is open to all European countries who are members of Uefa. England, Northern Ireland, Scotland and Wales refused to compete in the first European Championship, which had 17 countries participating. They were Austria, Bulgaria, Czechoslovakia, Denmark, France, East Germany, Greece, Hungary, Ireland, Norway, Poland, Portugal, Romania, Spain, Turkey, USSR and Yugoslavia. The first winners were the Soviet Union who beat Yugoslavia 2-1 in the Final, held in Paris, France on 10 July 1960 before just 17,966 fans. Soviet players scored all the goals – Metreveli and Ponedelnik scored in the correct goal, while Netto managed to put it into his own net. The competition was changed to its present name in 1968. No British team has reached the Final and no country has managed to retain the Championship title. West Germany came closest, winning in 1972 (the year the Olympics Games were also held in Munich) and 1980. The winners get the Henri Delaunay Cup; he was the first secretary-general of Uefa and died in 1955.

THE FIRST

PITCH INVASION
TO CELEBRATE A GOAL

SUNDERLAND V TOTTENHAM HOTSPUR AT ROKER PARK, SUNDERLAND, COUNTY DURHAM, ENGLAND, SATURDAY 4 MARCH 1961

Chasing the Double, Spurs were drawn away to Sunderland in the Quarter-Finals of the FA Cup. When Willy McPheat equalized for Sunderland in the second half, around 3,000 of the 61,326 spectators rushed onto the pitch to celebrate, holding up play for seven minutes. The event was such a novelty that the BBC covered it and commentator Alan Weekes described it 'as testimony to the great enthusiasm of fans in the north east for football'. Sadly for Sunderland, they lost the replay at White Hart Lane 5-0 on 8 March 1961 in front of 64,797 supporters. Fans had obviously invaded the pitch before this match, but usually in frustration or anger, or at the end of play. For example, on 24 January 1925 in a Division Two match between Derby County and Wolverhampton Wanderers at the Baseball Ground, the crowd stormed onto the pitch and a Wolves player was punched before the police and stewards were able to restore order.

THE FIRST

EUROPEAN CUP WINNERS'
CUP FINAL

RANGERS V FLORENCE AT IBROX PARK, 150 EDMISTON DRIVE, GLASGOW, LANARKSHIRE, SCOTLAND, WEDNESDAY 17 MAY 1961 (FIRST LEG); AT STADIO COMMUNALE, FLORENCE, ITALY, SATURDAY 27 MAY 1961 (SECOND LEG)

The European Cup Winners' Cup began in 1960–1961 with just ten clubs participating. Wolverhampton Wanderers and Rangers were Britain's entrants. The first winners were Florence who beat Rangers 4-1 on aggregate in the two-legged Final (Florence lost the Final the following year to Atlético Madrid who had refused to enter in the first year). In fact, Florence had not been the winners of the Italian cup the previous season but runners-up to Juventus who went into the European Cup, thus allowing a space for Florence in the new competition. Rangers beat Wolverhampton Wanderers in the Semi-Final to reach the final stage.

ANOTHER FIRST AND AN ONLY IN THIS MATCH:
The FIRST Scottish team to play in a European cup final • The ONLY European Cup Winners' Cup Final played over two legs

—•••—

THE FIRST
LEAGUE CUP FINAL
ROTHERHAM UNITED V ASTON VILLA AT MILLMOOR GROUND, ROTHERHAM, ENGLAND, TUESDAY 22 AUGUST 1961 (FIRST LEG); AT VILLA PARK, TRINITY ROAD, BIRMINGHAM, ENGLAND, TUESDAY 5 SEPTEMBER 1961 (SECOND LEG)

The League Cup began in 1960, but it would not be until 1967–1968 that all 92 Football League clubs entered. For the first competition Arsenal, Sheffield Wednesday, Tottenham Hotspur, West Bromwich Albion and Wolverhampton Wanderers refused to participate in what was called 'Hardaker's Folly' (after Football League secretary Alan Hardaker) because they said that they were already playing too many fixtures. Maurice Cook playing for Fulham against Bristol Rovers at Eastville Stadium scored **the FIRST League Cup goal** on 26 September 1960. Until 1967 the Final was a two-legged affair and the first Final First Leg was held at Millmoor when Rotherham beat Aston Villa 2-0. In the Second Leg Villa won 3-0 after extra time to become the first winners. In 1967 Uefa declared that the winners of the League Cup would get a place in the Fairs Cup, but only if they were in Division One, thus Division Three winners Queens Park Rangers (1967) and Swindon Town (1969) were denied their place in European competition. **The FIRST team to win the League Cup twice** was Tottenham Hotspur on 27 February 1971 (the year that deadly rivals Arsenal did the Double, so all the major trophies finished the 1970–1971 season in north London trophy cabinets) and in 1973.

ANOTHER FIRST IN THE FIRST LEG: The FIRST
League Cup Final goal was scored by Barry Webster of Rotherham

THE FIRST
BRITISH TEAM
TO COMPETE IN TWO
MAJOR EUROPEAN FINALS

BIRMINGHAM CITY V BARCELONA IN INTER-CITIES FAIRS CUP AT ST
ANDREWS, BIRMINGHAM, ENGLAND, TUESDAY 29 MARCH 1960 (FIRST
LEG); AT BARCELONA, SPAIN, WEDNESDAY 4 MAY 1960 (SECOND LEG);
V AS ROMA IN INTER-CITIES FAIRS CUP AT ST ANDREWS, BIRMINGHAM,
ENGLAND, WEDNESDAY 27 SEPTEMBER 1961 (FIRST LEG); AT ROME,
ITALY, WEDNESDAY 11 OCTOBER 1961 (SECOND LEG)

Birmingham City became the first English team to compete in two major
European Finals when they met AS Roma in their second consecutive
Fairs Cup Final. Sadly for the Blues, they lost on both occasions. In 1960
they lost to Barcelona 4-1 in Spain, having forced a goalless draw at home.
The following season they drew 2-2 in the First Leg at home and then lost
2-0 away.

THE ONLY
DIVISION FOUR TEAM
TO REACH A MAJOR CUP FINAL

Rochdale v Norwich City in League Cup at Spotland, Willbutts Lane,
Rochdale, Lancashire, England, Thursday 26 April 1962 (First Leg); at
Carrow Road, Norwich, Norfolk, England, Tuesday 1 May 1962 (Second Leg)

Rochdale made history in 1962 when they became the only Division Four
side to reach the Final of the League Cup. Sadly, there was no happy
ending to their fairy tale – they lost to Division Two Norwich 3-1 on
aggregate. Seven months earlier, another unique incident occurred in the
League Cup when the Final from the previous season, which had been
held over, was finally played, making it **the ONLY season with two
different finals of a major trophy**.

THE FIRST

PLAYER TO SCORE IN TWO
WORLD CUP FINALS

VAVÁ, BRAZIL V SWEDEN AT RAASUNDA STADIUM, SOLNA, SWEDEN, SUNDAY 29 JUNE 1958; BRAZIL V CZECHOSLOVAKIA AT ESTADIO NACIONAL, SANTIAGO, CHILE, SUNDAY 17 JUNE 1962

Vavá (Edvaldo Izídio Neto) of Brazil was the first player to score in two World Cup Finals. In 1958 he equalized in the ninth minute, four minutes after Sweden had taken the lead. With 32 minutes on the clock he gave Brazil the lead and the South Americans never looked back, winning 5-2. Four years later Vavá scored Brazil's third goal when they beat the Czechs 3-1. He played 20 times for Brazil and scored 15 goals. Born on the same day as murderer Charles Manson, on 12 November 1934, Vavá died in Rio de Janeiro on 19 January 2002.

THE LAST

BRITISH PLAYERS
JAILED FOR MATCH FIXING

Ipswich Town v Sheffield Wednesday at Portman Road, Ipswich, Suffolk, England, Saturday 1 December 1962

Jimmy Gauld was a little-known ex-footballer with a gambling problem. Having played for Charlton Athletic, Everton, Plymouth Argyle, Swindon Town, St Johnstone and Mansfield Town, his career had ended prematurely in 1959 with a broken leg. In late 1962 he asked David 'Bronco' Layne, a former teammate at Swindon Town, if he could suggest a game on which to place a bet. Layne, then at Sheffield Wednesday, said that his team were unlikely to beat Ipswich Town in the forthcoming fixture at Portman Road. Layne approached fellow players Peter Swan and wing half Tony Kay and suggested that they 'fix' the match. All three bet against their own side. Kay, who had played once for England and scored on his debut in an 8-1 victory over Switzerland and therefore could expect more appearances, placed a £50 wager. He said later, 'Layne approached me before the Ipswich game and said, "What do you reckon today?" I said, "Well, we've never won down here [Portman Road]." He said, "Give me £50 and I'll get you twice your money." I thought that was a good deal.' Wednesday lost 2–0. Not long after Tony Kay signed for Everton for £60,000, becoming Britain's most expensive footballer.

On 12 April 1964 Jimmy Gauld sold his story to the *Sunday People* for £7,000. In a Liverpool nightclub Kay was told, 'You're all over the front page of the *Sunday People* about the Ipswich game. They're saying you bet on the match and the bookmakers have been screaming because they lost £35,000 that week.' Kay remembered:

There had been rumours for ages about match fixing in football, but no one had ever proved it. Gauld knew Layne, who had been at Mansfield and who before the Ipswich match had acted as the go-between. I had never met Gauld, but then one day he turned up at my house in Liverpool and introduced himself as a friend of David Layne's. He said that he wanted to speak to me, so we went and sat in his car outside my house. He began to fire questions at me, trying to confuse me. He asked if I'd accepted money for fixing a game. I said, "I don't know what you're talking about." I didn't realize that he was recording our conversation. The tape of our conversation was used in court as evidence against me. It was one of the first times that this had ever happened. But even though the tape was incoherent and you could hear nothing, it still stood up.

KAY AND THE KRAYS

Following Tony Kay's release from an open prison near Leeds, where he served ten weeks, an associate of the Kray Twins approached him. The gruesome twosome wanted to learn all they could about taped evidence (which had done for Kay) and sent Kay a first-class rail ticket. The ex-footballer was too scared to decline and was wined and dined by the criminal pair. Kay had another brush with the law some time later when he was fined £400 for selling a fake diamond. He had fled to Spain when he heard the police were looking for him and eventually stayed there for 12 years. After four years on the run he 'sneaked back to Sheffield to see friends [and] I spent a weekend in the cells' before he was fined.

In 1965 the players came to trial. On 26 January Tony Kay was found guilty, fined £150, banned from playing football for life and sentenced to four months in prison. Peter Swan and David Layne were found guilty, as was Jimmy Gauld who was sent down for four years and fined £5,000. Also jailed were Mansfield players Brian Phillips and Sammy Chapman, along with Ronald Howells, Ken Thomson, Richard Beattie and Jack Fountain. Kay later said:

'Do I regret placing that bet? Well, I think I was harshly punished. I won only £150 from the bet, but my whole career was destroyed. They took away the game I loved and I have never really recovered from that.'

THE LAST
AMATEUR TO PLAY IN DIVISION ONE
MIKE PINNER, 1962–1963

Mike Pinner, a solicitor by trade, played in goal for Leyton Orient in the 1962–1963 season (the only year they spent in the top flight, being relegated at the end of the season). The Division One title went to Everton that year. Pinner played 77 times for the Os before moving to Lisburn Distillery in 1965 where he finished his playing career. He had also represented Great Britain in the 1960 summer Olympics and played 52 times for England's amateur side. At various times he was on the books of Cambridge University, Pegasus, Aston Villa, Corinthian-Casuals, Sheffield Wednesday, Queens Park Rangers, Manchester United (for whom he played four times in the 1960–1961 season, making his debut on 4 February 1961 in a 1-1 home draw against Aston Villa), Chelsea and Swansea City.

THE FIRST
POOLS PANEL
SATURDAY 26 JANUARY 1963

Many games were lost during the winter of 1962–1963, owing to the freezing weather that gripped most of Britain. Snow fell on Boxing Day

1962 and every match scheduled for New Year's Day was cancelled. The Third Round of the FA Cup was due to be played on 5 January 1963, but bad weather allowed just five to be played. So bad were the conditions that it was not until 11 March that the round was finished. The pools companies were worried and on 26 January 1963 the Pools Panel was empanelled by the Pool Promoters' Association to predict the results of matches for the first time. The original panel was Tom Finney, Tommy Lawton, Ted Drake, George Young, Arthur Ellis and 1st Baron Brabazon of Tara, who met behind closed doors at the Connaught Rooms in London to work out the results of 38 matches. Their deliberations were then announced live on BBC Television. (See 1923, page 60.)

THE FIRST

MATCH FOR ALF RAMSEY AS ENGLAND MANAGER

ENGLAND V FRANCE AT PARCS DES PRINCES, PARIS, FRANCE, WEDNESDAY 27 FEBRUARY 1963

Taking over from Walter Winterbottom as England's second manager, Alf Ramsey wanted to make an impression, which he did, although perhaps not in the way he expected. England were 3-0 down by half-time and despite goals from Bobby Smith and Bobby Tambling lost the match 5-2. To add to his woes, Ramsey's suitcase went missing on the flight and he had to spend the trip in the clothes he flew out in.

THE FIRST

FATHER AND SON TO WIN ENGLAND CAPS

GEORGE RICHARD EASTHAM, BOLTON WANDERERS, SUNDAY 18 MAY 1935/ACCRINGTON STANLEY, OCTOBER 1958; GEORGE EDWARD EASTHAM, STOKE CITY, WEDNESDAY 8 MAY 1963/STOKE CITY, MARCH 1977

George Richard, the father, was 20 years old when he played just one international against Holland on 18 May 1935 while he was with Bolton

Wanderers. He also played in the same Ards side as his son in the 1954–1955 season. He later became manager of Accrington Stanley in October 1958. George Edward, the son, was more successful, playing 19 times for England. He made his first appearance in an England shirt on 8 May 1963 against Brazil. He was part of the squad that won the 1966 World Cup, although his last appearance came on 3 July 1966 in a friendly against Denmark at Copenhagen before the tournament started. He became manager of Stoke City in March 1977. He lasted just ten months in the job before leaving and emigrating to South Africa to run a sportswear business.

THE GEORGE EASTHAMS WERE ALSO:
The ONLY father and son England internationals and League managers

THE FIRST

BRITISH TEAM TO WIN A MAJOR EUROPEAN TROPHY

TOTTENHAM HOTSPUR V ATLÉTICO MADRID IN EUROPEAN CUP WINNERS' CUP FINAL AT FEIJENOORD STADION, ROTTERDAM, HOLLAND, WEDNESDAY 15 MAY 1963

Beating the Spaniards of Atlético Madrid 5-1 gave Spurs the honour of being the first British team to win a major European trophy when they lifted the European Cup Winners' Cup. The goals came from Jimmy Greaves (two), who became **the First British player to score in two major European Finals**, John White and a brace from winger Terry Dyson, who also made two of the others. As the players celebrated in the dressing room, centre forward Bobby Smith approached Dyson with words of encouragement, 'Well done, Terry, fantastic son. If I were you, I'd f***** well retire now.'

THE FIRST

ENGLISH TEAMS TO MEET IN EUROPE

TOTTENHAM HOTSPUR V MANCHESTER UNITED IN THE EUROPEAN CUP WINNERS' CUP AT WHITE HART LANE, 748 HIGH ROAD, TOTTENHAM, LONDON, ENGLAND, TUESDAY 3 DECEMBER 1963

When Spurs (European Cup Winners' Cup holders) played Manchester United (FA Cup winners) at White Hart Lane it was the first time two English teams had met in a European competition. On this First Leg Spurs ran out comfortable winners by two goals to nil. The Second Leg at Old Trafford a week later was a different matter and the Red Devils thrashed Spurs 4-1 to go through 4-3 on aggregate. To add to the woes of the Lilywhites, not only were they out of the tournament but their captain Dave Mackay broke his leg in the match.

THE ONLY

PAPIER MÂCHÉ CHAMPIONSHIP TROPHY

Liverpool v Arsenal at Anfield, Seaforth, Liverpool, Lancashire, England, Saturday 18 April 1964

Bill Shankly's Liverpool needed to beat Arsenal in their final home match of the season to win the Division One title in 1963–1964 and duly and comprehensively did so, scoring 5-0 in front of the Kop with goalie Tommy Lawrence saving a George Eastham penalty. Ten minutes from time, Ian Callaghan missed a penalty and the chance to make it 6-0. It was Shankly's Liverpool's first Championship trophy and naturally they wanted to show it off to their fans, but the previous holders Merseyside rivals Everton refused to give it to Liverpool, insisting on following a rule that said that it must be returned to the Football League. Using Scouse initiative, an enterprising Liverpool fan had a trophy made up of papier mâché and it was this that Ron Yeats and the team paraded around Anfield. (See 1964, page 128.)

THE ONLY
TEAM TO LOSE THREE
FA CUP FINALS
HAVING BEEN IN THE LEAD IN THEM ALL

PRESTON NORTH END V SUNDERLAND AT WEMBLEY STADIUM, MIDDLESEX, ENGLAND, SATURDAY 1 MAY 1937; V WEST BROMWICH ALBION AT WEMBLEY STADIUM, MIDDLESEX, ENGLAND, SATURDAY 1 MAY 1954; V WEST HAM UNITED AT WEMBLEY STADIUM, MIDDLESEX, ENGLAND, SATURDAY 2 MAY 1964

It looked as if Preston North End would beat West Ham in the 1964 FA Cup Final, but the Hammers had other ideas. A last-minute winner saw Bobby Moore and not Nobby Lawton lift the trophy. It was for Preston the third time they had seen victory grasped from their hands. They had been in the lead in 1937 against Sunderland and lost 3-1, and had been in a similar position 17 years later against West Brom before surrendering and losing 3-2.

THE ONLY
DIVISION ONE FOOTBALLER
KILLED BY LIGHTNING

John White, Enfield, Middlesex, England, Tuesday 21 July 1964

Tottenham Hotspur and Scotland international John White was on Crews Hill Golf Course, Enfield, Middlesex in the summer of 1964 when a storm began. He took shelter under a tree and was instantly killed when struck by lightning. He was 27.

THEME OF THE DAY

The current theme tune to *Match of the Day*, written by Barry Stoller, was introduced in 1970. From 1964 until 1970 the theme used was one called 'Drum Majorette' and was composed by Major Leslie Statham, the leader of the band of the Welsh Guards.

THE ONLY
MATCH FEATURED ON
THE FIRST EDITION OF
MATCH OF THE DAY

LIVERPOOL V ARSENAL AT ANFIELD, SEAFORTH, LIVERPOOL, LANCASHIRE, ENGLAND, 6.30 PM SATURDAY 22 AUGUST 1964

The BBC's flagship football programme began on BBC2 with a thrilling match between Liverpool and Arsenal at Anfield. Fewer than 20,000 people saw the Reds of Merseyside beat the Reds of north London by three goals to two on television because BBC2 was then only available in the London area. Unlike today, there was only one match on the programme, which was presented by Kenneth Wolstenholme. He began the first show with the words, 'Welcome to *Match of the Day*, the first of a weekly series on BBC2. This afternoon we are in Beatleville.'

THE ONLY
TRANSFER COMPLETED IN THE
HOUSES OF PARLIAMENT

IAN LAWTHER, SCUNTHORPE UNITED TO BRENTFORD, AT HOUSES OF PARLIAMENT, LONDON, ENGLAND, NOVEMBER 1964

Born in Belfast, Ian Lawther was signed by Manchester United when he was 15, but was so homesick he went back to Northern Ireland and signed for Crusaders. In 1959 he signed for Sunderland and made his debut at Villa Park in a 3-0 defeat by Aston Villa on 31 August. On 26 October 1960 Lawther scored Sunderland's first goal in the League Cup in a 4-3 defeat at Brentford. His last match for Sunderland was a goalless draw away to Rotherham United on 11 March 1961. In the summer of that year he joined Blackburn Rovers for £18,000 to replace Derek Dougan, who had been sold to Aston Villa for £20,000. Sunderland spent £45,000 to replace Lawther with a centre forward named Brian Clough. After two years Lawther signed for Division Two Scunthorpe United in a £12,000 deal. In November 1964 he signed for Brentford in the Houses of Parliament – the Bees chairman was MP Jack Dunnett (Labour, Nottingham Central), who provided a gold pen for the occasion. In 1968 he signed for Halifax Town and then joined Stockport County where, in January 1973, he was sent off in the FA Cup for retaliating against Terry Neill, player-manager of Hull City. When he retired Lawther became a tailor in Halifax.

THE FIRST
SCOTTISH CAPTAINS
IN AN FA CUP FINAL
RON YEATS (LIVERPOOL) V BOBBY COLLINS (LEEDS UNITED)
AT WEMBLEY STADIUM, MIDDLESEX, ENGLAND,
SATURDAY 1 MAY 1965

For the first time in the FA Cup Final Scots captained both teams in 1965. It was the 84th final and the 37th played at Wembley. Neither team had won the trophy before. It was the first season in top flight for Leeds, following their winning the Division Two title in 1963–1964. Liverpool had been League champions in that season, but finished 1964–1965 in seventh place, five spots below Leeds. Liverpool were captained by Aberdeen-born Ron 'Rowdy' Yeats who had joined the Anfield club on 22 July 1961 from Dundee United. He stayed there for ten years before Bill Shankly sold him on 30 December 1971. Govanhill-born Bobby Collins joined Leeds in 1962 and three years later was named Footballer of the Year. Their nationality was about all the captains had in common. Yeats stood nearly 6 ft 2 in (1.88 m) high, while Bobby Collins barely made 5 ft 3 in (1.60 m); Yeats played in defence, while Collins patrolled the midfield. The match finished goalless at 90 minutes and became the first final since 1947 to require extra time. Roger Hunt scored the first goal of the game in the 93rd minute, only for Billy Bremner to equalize for Leeds two minutes later. With seven minutes left on the clock Ian St John headed Liverpool's winner.

THIS WAS ALSO: The FIRST FA Cup Final to feature a black player, Albert Johanneson (1940–1995)

THE FIRST
LEAGUE SUBSTITUTE
KEITH PEACOCK, CHARLTON ATHLETIC V BOLTON WANDERERS AT BURNDEN PARK, BOLTON, LANCASHIRE, ENGLAND, SATURDAY 21 AUGUST 1965

Keith Peacock, Division Two Charlton's midfielder, made history when he became the first substitute in the Football League, replacing injured goalkeeper Mike Rose after 11 minutes. John Hewie donned Rose's green top while Peacock took Hewie's place in defence. Peacock had joined the Addicks three years earlier and spent his entire career there, retiring in 1979 after 532 first team appearances. The Football League had initially agreed to one injured player being replaced, but it soon became apparent that it was impossible for referees to decide if a player was genuinely injured. From the start of the 1967–1968 season this rule was relaxed to

---

IMPROPER SUBSTITUTION
The FIRST substitute in football actually occurred on 20 January 1917 at Firhill, when a player called Morgan came on for the injured Morrison of Partick Thistle after five minutes of a match against Rangers. However, this was unauthorized and the Scottish League did not agree to substitutions until 1966.

allow substitutions for tactical reasons. **The First substitute in Scottish football** was Archie Gemmill of St Mirren, who replaced Jim Clunie after 23 minutes of a League Cup tie against Clyde on 13 August 1966. Eleven days later Paul Conn became **the First substitute in a Scottish League match**, playing for Queen's Park against Albion Rovers in a Division Two match.

THE FIRST
LEAGUE SUBSTITUTE TO SCORE A GOAL

BOB KNOX, BARROW V WREXHAM AT HOLKER STREET, BARROW-IN-FURNESS, CUMBRIA, ENGLAND, SATURDAY 21 AUGUST 1965

In August of the 1965–1966 season Bob Knox became the first substitute to score a League goal when his team Barrow won 4-2 against Wrexham.

BOB KNOX WAS ALSO: The FIRST League substitute to save a penalty when on 27 December 1965 he went between the sticks to replace injured goalkeeper Ken Mulholland in Barrow's 1-0 victory at Doncaster Rovers

THE FIRST
THEFT OF THE WORLD CUP

METHODIST CENTRAL HALL, STOREY'S GATE, LONDON, ENGLAND, SUNDAY 20 MARCH 1966

The Jules Rimet Trophy was designed by Abel Lafleur and made of gold-plated sterling silver on a blue base of lapis lazuli; it stood 13½ in (34.8 cm) high and weighed 8.3 lb (3.76 kg). It had had a chequered history before it came to England for the 1966 competition. Won by Italy in 1938, it spent the war years in a shoebox under the bed of Ottorino Barassi, the Italian vice-president of Fifa, to keep it safe from the Germans. On 18 March 1966 the Jules Rimet Trophy made its first public appearance in England on display on the Stanley Gibbons stand at Stampex, Britain's national stamp exhibition, at the Methodist Central Hall, Westminster. The World Cup was insured for £30,000, although its value was only £3,000.

At 12.10 pm on Sunday 20 March Alsa-Guard, the private security company hired to look after it, noticed that the trophy had been stolen. A nationwide hunt began and a petty crook called Edward Walter Betchley contacted the police, claiming to have the trophy and asking for £15,000 in used notes. But when he was arrested he insisted that he was only the go-between for a mystery man known only as 'The Pole'. At his trial on 8 July 1966 Betchley was sent to prison for two years for demanding money with menaces and intent to steal. He died in 1969 shortly after his release.

In case the World Cup was not to be found, the FA and Chelsea chairman Joe Mears asked Fifa president Sir Stanley Rous if a replica could be made. Fifa refused, but the FA secretly arranged for a gilded bronze replica to be made by George Bird of Alexander Clarke and Co.

A week after the theft the trophy was found in the front garden of 26-year-old Thames lighterman Dave Corbett, of 50, Beulah Hill, Upper Norwood, south London. Despite the stories, Pickles, a one-year-old black and white Border Collie, didn't find the trophy. Corbett said, 'Although Pickles sort of led me in the direction of the cup, it was me who found it. There were all these stories at the time that he dug it up from under a bush. Well, it wasn't quite like that.' Corbett took the trophy to Gipsy Hill police station where his statement revealed:

'Just as we were about to go out of the gate, I was putting the lead on the dog when I saw a package at the side of a bush. It was wrapped in newspaper. I stooped down to pick it up, and felt it was heavy. I had read in the papers about the World Cup, and seen pictures. Although I could not believe it possible I went indoors for a better look. Then I felt sure it was the Cup, and I told my wife I was going to the police station at Gipsy Hill, and went there straight away.'

He and the Cup were taken to Cannon Row station where Harold Mayes, an FA official, identified it. Neither David Corbett nor Pickles received any formal reward from the FA, not even a letter of thanks, but various other monetary sums made to Corbett totalled £6,000 – six times the amount the England team won for winning the trophy. Corbett bought a house in Lingfield, Surrey for £3,100, where he lives today. Pickles was given a year's supply of dog food for his part in the recovery,

---

JULES RIMET – WHO HE?

A French lawyer born in Theuley-les-Lavoncourt on 14 October 1873, Jules Rimet was the president of the French Football Federation from 1919 to 1945 and of Fifa from 1921 to 1954. He died on 16 October 1956.

---

but died in 1967 when he was strangled by his own lead while chasing a rabbit. He is buried in Corbett's back garden.

Although Bobby Moore hoisted the genuine trophy on 30 July 1966 when England beat West Germany 4-2, a policeman was charged with slipping into the home side's dressing room and replacing the real trophy with the worthless copy. The Jules Rimet Trophy was taken from Nobby Stiles and the midfielder handed the replica. It was the replica that was most often seen in public until it travelled to Mexico for the 1970 tournament when Brazil won it outright with their third win. On 20 December 1983 in Rio de Janeiro the Jules Rimet Trophy was again stolen and never recovered. The replica was sold at an auction in 1997 for £254,500. Fifa bought it anonymously and donated it to the English National Football Museum in Preston.

THE ONLY
PLAYER IN SIX
EUROPEAN CUP-WINNING SIDES

Francisco Gento, Real Madrid v Stade de Reims-Champagne at Parc des Princes, Paris, France, Wednesday 13 June 1956; Real Madrid v Fiorentina at Santiago Bernabéu, Madrid, Spain, Thursday 30 May 1957; Real Madrid v AC Milan at Stade du Heysel, Brussels, Belgium, Wednesday 28 May 1958; Real Madrid v Stade de Reims-Champagne at Nekardstadion, Stuttgart, Germany, Tuesday 2 June 1959; Real Madrid v Eintracht Frankfurt at Hampden Park, Mount Florida, Glasgow, Lanarkshire, Scotland, Wednesday 18 May 1960; Real Madrid v Partizan Belgrade at Stade du Heysel, Brussels, Belgium, Wednesday 11 May 1966

Franciso Gento joined Real Madrid in 1953 and until his retirement in 1971 played 428 times and won 43 caps for Spain. An outside left, he was nicknamed La Galerna del Cantábrico ('The Storm of Cantabria') and appeared in a dozen League-winning teams, two Spanish Cups and an unprecedented six European Cup-winning sides.

THE FIRST
ENGLAND FAILURE
TO SCORE AT WEMBLEY
England v Uruguay at Wembley Stadium, Middlesex, England, 7.30 pm Monday 11 July 1966

In the opening match of the 1966 World Cup England faced Uruguay, who had won the competition twice (1930 and 1950) and were ranked the 12th best team in the world. The match ended in a goalless draw before 87,148 spectators – the first time England had failed to score in an international at Wembley. It was the 25th occasion on which Bobby Moore had captained the side. The match marked the 20th and last England appearance for Manchester United's winger John Connelly.

THE FIRST
PROFESSIONAL PLAYER
SENT OFF AT WEMBLEY
ANTONIO RATTÍN, ARGENTINA V ENGLAND AT WEMBLEY STADIUM, MIDDLESEX, ENGLAND, 3 PM SATURDAY 23 JULY 1966

England drew Argentina in the Quarter-Finals of the World Cup and it was a bad-tempered match. Eventually, the West German referee Rudolf Kreitlein sent off Rattín, the Argentine captain, for dissent. Rattín, wearing the number ten shirt, refused to leave the pitch and only did so after eight minutes and discussions with three policemen, who persuaded him that sitting on the touchline would not be a good idea. As he walked to the dressing room he rumpled an England pennant on a midway flag. England won by a header on 78 minutes from Geoff Hurst, replacing the injured Jimmy Greaves who had appeared in all three of England's group matches. As Herr Kreitlein blew the final whistle England manager Alf Ramsey ran onto the pitch to stop George Cohen exchanging shirts with Alberto González who, bemused, wandered off and swapped with Ray Wilson. Ramsey later commented, 'Our best football will come against the right type of opposition – a team who come to play football, and not act as animals.'

THE ONLY
PLAYER TO SCORE A HAT-TRICK
IN A WORLD CUP FINAL
GEOFF HURST, ENGLAND V WEST GERMANY AT WEMBLEY STADIUM, MIDDLESEX, ENGLAND, SATURDAY 30 JULY 1966

Having beaten the 'animals' of Argentina, Alf Ramsey's England side prepared to face old enemy West Germany in the Final at Wembley. Lining his men up in a 4-4-2 formation, meaning that they played without wingers, England fell behind after 12 minutes from a strike by Helmut Haller. On 18 minutes England captain Bobby Moore was fouled and took a quick free kick, finding Hurst who headed home past Hans Tilkowski in the West German goal. The match was level after 45 minutes, but 32 minutes into the second half England went into the lead. Alan Ball took a corner on the right, finding Hurst, whose shot was deflected on to Martin Peters who made no mistake. England looked victory in the face, only for the West Germans to equalize through Wolfgang Weber.

In the first half of extra time England took the lead with a goal that rankles the Germans to this day. 'That man again' Alan Ball passed to Hurst, who struck the ball with his right foot, losing his balance as he did. The ball swept past Tilkowski, hit the underside of the crossbar and bounced down before Weber headed the ball away for a corner. Roger Hunt, who was closest to the West German goal, immediately turned round and began celebrating, but the Teutonic team claimed that the ball hadn't completely crossed the line. Swiss referee Gottfried Dienst went over to his Azerbaijani linesman Tofik Bakhramov, who told him that the ball had indeed crossed the line – 3-2 to England. The West Germans began to argue and berate the linesman, who spoke Russian, Turkish and Azeri, but not German. In the intervening years both referee and linesman have continued to insist that their decision was correct.

With just seconds remaining and the whistle in the referee's mouth, Bobby Moore cleared the ball to Geoff Hurst, who ran towards the opposition goal as spectators ran onto the pitch. He later confessed that he just kicked it as hard as he could, hoping to waste time. In fact, he hit a perfect shot that gave Tilkowski no chance. Commentating on the game for the BBC, Kenneth Wolstenholme said, 'Some people are on the pitch. They think it's all over' and then as Hurst scored, 'it is now. It's four.' There was no time for the game to restart and HM the Queen presented the Jules Rimet Trophy to Bobby Moore. (See below and 1968, page 143.)

THE ONLY

CAPTAIN TO LIFT THREE
MAJOR TROPHIES
IN THREE CONSECUTIVE SEASONS

BOBBY MOORE, WEST HAM UNITED V PRESTON NORTH END AT WEMBLEY STADIUM, MIDDLESEX, ENGLAND, 3PM SATURDAY 2 MAY 1964; WEST HAM UNITED V MUNICH 1860 AT WEMBLEY STADIUM, MIDDLESEX, ENGLAND, WEDNESDAY 19 MAY 1965; ENGLAND V WEST GERMANY AT WEMBLEY STADIUM, MIDDLESEX, ENGLAND, SATURDAY 30 JULY 1966

Bobby Moore, the handsome, blond skipper of West Ham and England, is the only captain to win three separate major trophies in three consecutive seasons – and all the presentations took part at Wembley. In 1964 he captained West Ham to a 3-2 victory in the FA Cup Final against Preston North End. The Hammers' goals came from John Sissons, Geoff Hurst and Ronnie Boyce. The following season Moore led them to victory against the Germans of Munich 1860 in the European Cup Winners' Cup Final, beating them 2-0 with both goals coming from Alan Sealey. In winning the ECWC West Ham fielded a team of 11 Englishmen. The

Germans had nine natives and two Yugoslavs. Just over a year later Moore became **the ONLY England captain to lift the World Cup** when England beat West Germany 4-2.

THE FIRST

PLAYER SOLD FOR A SIX-FIGURE TRANSFER FEE BETWEEN ENGLISH CLUBS

ALAN BALL, BLACKPOOL TO EVERTON, ENGLAND, MONDAY 15 AUGUST 1966

The month after the squeaky-voiced redhead won a World Cup winner's medal, Alan Ball signed for Everton from Blackpool for £112,000 in the first six-figure transfer between English clubs. On 22 December 1971 Arsenal manager Bertie Mee paid a record-breaking £220,000 to bring midfield dynamo Ball to Highbury. He became club captain in 1974, but two years later he didn't fit in with new manager Terry Neill's vision and was sold in December 1976 to Southampton. On 25 April 2007 Ball died aged 61 of a heart attack while trying to put out a bonfire at his home in Warsash, Hampshire. He was the second member of the World Cup-winning team to die. (See 1983, page 177.)

THE FIRST

PLAYER SENT OFF IN A HOME INTERNATIONAL

BILLY FERGUSON, NORTHERN IRELAND V ENGLAND AT WINDSOR PARK, DONEGALL AVENUE, BELFAST, COUNTY ANTRIM, NORTHERN IRELAND, THURSDAY 20 OCTOBER 1966

In front of 48,600 spectators Billy Ferguson of Linfield was the first player from any country to be sent off during a Home International at Windsor Park after fouling England number seven Alan Ball when Northern Ireland lost 2-0 to England. The match also doubled as a qualifier for the 1968 European Championships.

BILLY FERGUSON WAS ALSO: The FIRST Northern
Ireland player sent off in an international

THE FIRST
FA CUP MATCH ON CCTV
**EVERTON V LIVERPOOL AT GOODISON PARK, LIVERPOOL,
LANCASHIRE, ENGLAND, SATURDAY 11 MARCH 1967**

The Merseyside derby is always a sell-out and this match was no exception. A grand total of 64,851 fans paid to watch the match live at Goodison, while another 40,109 went to Anfield, where they handed over their hard-earned cash to watch the match on big screens. Everton won the match thanks to a solitary effort from Alan Ball two minutes into stoppage time in the first half.

THE FIRST
BRITISH CLUB IN THE WORLD CLUB CHAMPIONSHIP
CELTIC V RACING CLUB OF ARGENTINA AT HAMPDEN PARK, MOUNT
FLORIDA, GLASGOW, LANARKSHIRE, SCOTLAND, WEDNESDAY
18 OCTOBER 1967 (FIRST LEG); AT AVELLANEDA, BUENOS AIRES, ARGENTINA,
WEDNESDAY 1 NOVEMBER 1967 (SECOND LEG); AT ESTADIO CENTENARIO,
MONTEVIDEO, URUGUAY, SATURDAY 4 NOVEMBER 1967 (DECIDER)

The World Club Championship was designed in 1958 to pit the champions of Europe against the champions of South America. An initial problem was that South America did not have any way of deciding who the champion team was, so they invented the Copa Libertadores. The first winners were Peñarol of Uruguay and they met Real Madrid in **the FIRST World Club Championship** in 1960. The winners were the Spaniards, who won 5-1 on aggregate. It would be seven years before a British team played in the World Club Championship. Celtic, winners of the European Cup, met Racing Club of Argentina, which many neutrals and all of one half of Glasgow felt would be more at home in a boxing ring than on a football pitch. Celtic won the First Leg 1-0, although they played at Hampden Park and not their own ground. The Second Leg in Argentina began in disaster – Ronnie Simpson, Celtic's goalie, was knocked unconscious by a weapon thrown from the crowd before the match began and was replaced by John Fallon. It then ended in farce, following a 2-1 victory for the violent Racing Club – there was no away goals rule to give Celtic the trophy and Fifa refused to countenance both teams holding the honour for six months each.

A third match was arranged three days later at supposedly neutral Montevideo, Uruguay. It was one of the most horrific episodes ever to take place on a football pitch. Celtic chairman Bob Kelly didn't want the match to go ahead, but manager Jock Stein was insistent that his side could win. Celtic demanded the referee be changed and assurances for their own security before agreeing to play. The Celtic players had been kept awake on the night before the match by constant chanting from Argentinian supporters who had made the journey to Uruguay. Almost as soon as the decider began the South Americans started kicking and hacking the Celtic players. The Paraguay referee Rodolfo Pérez Osorio seemed unable to get a grip and maintain control. At one stage in the middle of the first half he called both captains together to get them to instil some discipline into their teams. It didn't work. There were 30 fouls given against Celtic and 21 against Racing Club. Six players were sent off – four from Celtic and two from Racing Club – although only five left the field of play. Bertie Auld refused to leave the pitch and the referee didn't insist.

FRANCIS THÉBAUD REPORTING FOR **MIRROIR DE FOOTBALL** WROTE OF JIMMY JOHNSTONE'S DISMISSAL: **Johnstone, in the middle of the pitch, slid the ball to Wallace and got free to receive the return. Martín without bothering about the ball threw himself at Johnstone's waist. Both fell and Johnstone struggled and Martín rolled on the ground as if he had been the victim of a blow. Without hesitating, Peréz sent Johnstone off! Thus he who had been the constant target of all the aggression since the beginning of the match... became the victim of a man whose aim was to protect the footballer against the fakers and the foulers. For my part, I have never seen such a staggering decision.**

Juan Carlos Cárdenas scored the only goal of the game in the 56th minute for Racing Club. Even the Uruguayans in the crowd were unimpressed by their Latin American neighbours, and as Racing Club tried to do a lap of honour, they were pelted by whatever the spectators could get their hands on. In Argentina the newspaper *La Racon* headlined their report, 'Racing have recovered the glory days of our football!' However, in Uruguay *El Día* said, 'This was no football, it was a disgrace... The match was a farce and a fraud.' Celtic fined their players £250 for their disgraceful behaviour. For the Argentinians' appalling actions they were each rewarded with £2,000 and a new car. In December 1979 Racing Club goalie Agustin Mario Cejas gave an interview in which he expressed his opinion of that night:

'A fairly normal match for us. I was given a "pacific" role. I didn't have to hit anybody, just be goalkeeper. But suddenly, Basile really hit the redhead Johnstone with a hell of a foul, one of the most violent I've ever seen. And the referee sent Basile off. I started walking casually out of my goal with my hands behind my back, and made my way slowly towards Johnstone. He was still on the ground when I arrived, so I kicked him as hard as I could for getting my teammate sent off.'

—•◦•—

THE FIRST
SUBSTITUTE IN AN FA CUP FINAL
Dennis Clarke, West Bromwich Albion v Everton at Wembley Stadium, Middlesex, England, Saturday 18 May 1968

John Kaye was the first player substituted in an FA Cup Final when Throstles manager Alan Ashman pulled off the centre half and replaced him with Dennis Clarke, another centre half. With just four minutes to go, Everton's Johnny Morrisey crossed and found Jimmy Husband unmarked on the six-yard box. Rather than achieving fame, Husband managed to head the ball over and the game went into extra time. West Brom won the Cup for the fifth time, beating Everton 1-0, when Jeff Astle scored the only goal of the game three minutes into extra time and become the first player since Jackie Milburn in 1951 to score in every round.

OTHER FIRSTS AND A LAST IN THIS MATCH:
The FIRST FA Cup Final televised in colour • The FIRST FA Cup Final at which a six-figure sum (£110,000) was taken in gate money • The LAST FA Cup win, to date, for West Bromwich Albion

---

GOAL SUBSTITUTE

Each team was allowed one substitute and oddly Matt Busby chose reserve goalie Jimmy Rimmer as his sole replacement player.

THE FIRST
ENGLISH CLUB TO WIN THE
EUROPEAN CUP

MANCHESTER UNITED V BENFICA AT WEMBLEY STADIUM, MIDDLESEX, ENGLAND, WEDNESDAY 29 MAY 1968

Manchester United beat the Portuguese champions after extra time to win the 13th European Cup. Playing in an unfamiliar all-blue strip, United were unable to break down Benfica's defences in the first half, but with eight minutes of the second half gone captain Bobby Charlton opened United's account with a rare header. On 75 minutes Jaime Graça scored for Benfica and that was the score when the Italian referee Concetto Lo Bello signalled the end of 90 minutes. Just three minutes into extra time George Best put United in the lead again and Brian Kidd (replacing the injured Denis Law) made it three a minute later. On 99 minutes Bobby Charlton added his second to put the game beyond Benfica's reach. A year after Celtic became **the FIRST British team to win the European Cup** (they beat Inter Milan 2-1 at Lisbon), Manchester United became the first English club to lift the trophy.

THE FIRST
ENGLAND PLAYER SENT OFF
IN A FULL INTERNATIONAL

ALAN MULLERY, ENGLAND V YUGOSLAVIA AT STADIO COMMUNALE, FLORENCE, ITALY, WEDNESDAY 5 JUNE 1968

The World Cup winners met Yugoslavia in the European Championship in Italy hoping to win the competition to add to the Jules Rimet Trophy. It was not to be and Spurs wing half, Mullery, became the first England player sent off in a full international after he kicked out at the Yugoslav player Dobrivoje Trivic, who late tackled him. The match was violent, although there was only one sending-off and two bookings (Roger Hunt went into the book for England). Norman Hunter put Ivan Osim out of the game with a crunching tackle. A goal from captain Dragan Dzajic settled the match against England. **The FIRST England player sent off in England** was Paul Scholes of Manchester United in a European Championship qualifying match against Sweden on 5 June 1999 at Wembley.

THE FIRST
BRITISH CLUB TO WIN THE
INTER-CITIES FAIRS CUP

LEEDS UNITED V FERENCVAROS AT ELLAND ROAD, LEEDS, WEST YORKSHIRE, ENGLAND, WEDNESDAY 7 AUGUST 1968 (FIRST LEG); IN BUDAPEST, HUNGARY, WEDNESDAY 11 SEPTEMBER 1968 (SECOND LEG)

The 10th Inter-Cities Fairs Cup was the first to come to Britain when Leeds United defeated Ferencvaros of Hungary, having lost in the Final the previous year to Dinamo Zagreb 2-0 on aggregate. In the First Leg at home Leeds scored just one goal, but with the Second Leg a goalless draw it was enough to bring the Cup to Elland Road. Leeds also became **the FIRST British club to win a European trophy without losing a match**.

THE FIRST
ENGLISH CLUB IN THE
WORLD CLUB CHAMPIONSHIP

MANCHESTER UNITED V ESTUDIANTES DE LA PLATA AT BOCA JUNIORS STADIUM, BUENOS AIRES, ARGENTINA, WEDNESDAY 25 SEPTEMBER 1968 (FIRST LEG); AT OLD TRAFFORD, MANCHESTER, ENGLAND, 7.45 PM WEDNESDAY 16 OCTOBER 1968 (SECOND LEG)

A year after Celtic lost to Racing Club of Argentina in a match that descended into a punch-up, Manchester United faced a similar barrage of assaults from their Argentinian opponents Estudiantes. The South Americans won the First Leg by a solitary goal and then travelled to Old Trafford for the Second Leg. Like their compatriots a year earlier, Estudiantes were in no mind to play football. Bobby Charlton had to have several stitches in a wound caused by a vicious tackle. Little Nobby Stiles was headbutted and later sent off for dissent by the referee. Denis Law was carried off the pitch on a stretcher and George Best was sent off after retaliating following a foul on him by José Hugo Medina, who was also dismissed. The match ended with a goal apiece (Willie Morgan scored for United), which meant for the second year in a row against a British opponent the Argentines had returned home with the trophy. In 1999 United beat Palmeiras 1-0 to become **the ONLY British side to win the World Club Championship**.

THE LAST

PLAYER TO DATE TO SCORE
SIX GOALS IN A LEAGUE MATCH

Geoff Hurst, West Ham United v Sunderland at Boleyn Ground, Green Street, Upton Park, London, England, Saturday 19 October 1968

The ONLY man to score a hat-trick in a World Cup Final was also the last player to date to hit a double hat-trick in a Football League match. Geoff Hurst scored six of his team's eight goals as they thrashed Sunderland 8-0 in a Division One match. Sunderland player Martin Harvey moaned, 'We were so gutted, we attended the post-match buffet and ate nothing.' Hurst later admitted that he had used his hand to score the first as he dived on the referee's blindside. (See 1966, page 135).

THE FIRST

FOOTBALL SONG AT NUMBER ONE
'BACK HOME', ENGLAND 1970 WORLD CUP SQUAD, SATURDAY 16 MAY 1970

The first song by a football team to top the hit parade was the England 1970 World Cup song *Back Home*. Written and produced by Scottish

Bill Martin and Irish Phil Coulter, with a ditty called *Cinnamon Stick* on the B-side, it entered the charts on 18 April 1970, reaching the top spot five weeks later on 16 May. It spent three weeks at the top of the hit parade and 17 weeks in the charts. The England team even appeared on *Top of the Pops* to sing their anthem, clad in tuxedos.

THE FIRST
FATHER AND SON
TO APPEAR IN THE WORLD CUP

Martín Vantolrá, Spain v Italy at Giovanni Berta, Florence, Italy, Friday 1 June 1934 (first World Cup match); José Vantolrá, Mexico v Union of Soviet Socialist Republics at Estadio Azteca, Mexico City, Mexico, Sunday 31 May 1970 (first World Cup match)

The first father and son to both play in the World Cup oddly played for different countries. Having beaten Brazil 3-1 in their opening match, Spain drew with Italy. In the replay Martín Vantolrá made his first appearance in the 1934 Finals, but was unable to prevent Italy winning 1-0. It was 36 years later, almost to the day, that his son José played his first match for Mexico. He played in all four games in the 1970 tournament as Mexico were knocked out 4-1 by Italy in the Quarter-Finals.

THE ONLY
GRANDFATHER AND GRANDSON
TO APPEAR IN THE WORLD CUP

LUIS PÉREZ, MEXICO V FRANCE AT ESTADIO POCITOS, MONTEVIDEO, URUGUAY, 3 PM SUNDAY 13 JULY 1930 (FIRST WORLD CUP MATCH); MARIO PÉREZ, MEXICO V UNION OF SOVIET SOCIALIST REPUBLICS AT ESTADIO AZTECA, MEXICO CITY, MEXICO, SUNDAY 31 MAY 1970 (FIRST WORLD CUP MATCH)

Luis Pérez appeared in the first match in the World Cup (against France) and in two of Mexico's three matches, all of which they lost. The match in which José Vantolrá became the first son to follow his father into the

World Cup was also the same match that Mario Pérez became the first grandson to follow his grandfather into the tournament, although this time representing the same country. Pérez played in all four games in the 1970 tournament.

—•••—

THE FIRST
YELLOW CARD

EVGENY LOVCHEV, UNION OF SOVIET SOCIALIST REPUBLICS V MEXICO AT ESTADIO AZTECA, MEXICO CITY, MEXICO, SUNDAY 31 MAY 1970

The yellow and red cards to signify bookings and sendings-off were invented by former referee Ken Aston. In 1962 he had been the referee during the match between Chile and Italy and needed an armed guard to get off the pitch. Four years later he watched in dismay as the Argentinians surrounded the West German referee Rudolf Kreitlein after he sent off their captain Antonio Rattín for 'violence of the tongue', even though neither man could understand the other. The next day Aston found that the Charlton brothers had both been booked, but neither knew. As he drove his MG home from his office one day he got his eureka moment when he was caught at traffic lights. Fifa introduced the red and yellow cards in time for the 1970 World Cup. In the opening match Soviet defender Evgeny Lovchev became the first player shown a yellow card. Four other players followed him into the referee's notebook, but not one red card was shown at the tournament. (See 1974, page 156).

—•••—

THE FIRST
MATCH DECIDED ON PENALTIES

HULL CITY V MANCHESTER UNITED AT BOOTHFERRY PARK, HULL, EAST YORKSHIRE, ENGLAND, WEDNESDAY 5 AUGUST 1970

The first match decided on penalties in England was the Semi-Final of the Watney Cup between Hull City and Manchester United. At 120 minutes the score stood at 1-1 and United ended up winning 4-3 on penalties. George Best was the first to take a penalty and score, as did the next five takers. Denis Law was the first to miss, his shot being saved by former Arsenal keeper Ian McKechnie in the Hull goal. However, Hull missed their next two attempts (including one by McKechnie who skyed the ball over the bar) and United made their way to the Final (the first of only four Watney Cup Finals), where they lost 4-1 to Derby County at the Baseball Ground.

THE FIRST
SUBSTITUTE TO SCORE IN AN FA CUP FINAL

EDDIE KELLY, ARSENAL V LIVERPOOL AT WEMBLEY STADIUM, MIDDLESEX, ENGLAND, SATURDAY 8 MAY 1971

Arsenal sniffed the possibility of winning their first Double in 1971. The teams met before a full house of 100,000 at Wembley, with Arsenal wearing their change strip of gold and blue and Liverpool their familiar all red. Arsenal ran out 2-1 winners after a heat-sapping extra time with the goals coming from Eddie Kelly, who had replaced Peter Storey, and Charlie George. Years later Peter Thompson of Liverpool recalled his manager Bill Shankly's pre-match team talk: 'He really didn't give Arsenal any credit. He said, "They're nothing to beat, these Cockneys from London."'

THE FIRST
CLUB TO WIN THE INTER-CITIES FAIRS CUP WITHOUT WINNING THE FINAL

LEEDS UNITED V JUVENTUS AT STADIO COMMUNALE, TURIN, ITALY, WEDNESDAY 26 MAY 1971 (FIRST LEG); AT STADIO COMMUNALE, TURIN, ITALY, FRIDAY 28 MAY 1971 (RESCHEDULED FIRST LEG); AT ELLAND ROAD, LEEDS, WEST YORKSHIRE, ENGLAND, THURSDAY 3 JUNE 1971 (SECOND LEG)

Leeds won the Fairs Cup for the second time in 1971, but didn't actually score any more goals than their opponents. The first match at Turin was

CAPELLO'S CONTRIBUTION

A promising young chap called Fabio Capello scored Juventus's second goal in the rescheduled First Leg in the 55th minute.

abandoned after 51 minutes because of torrential rain with the score at 0-0. Two days later the teams tried again and managed to complete the 90 minutes in a 2-2 draw. Paul Madeley and substitute Mick Bates scored the goals for Leeds. Just under a week later the two teams met again and this time the match ended in a one-all draw, with Allan Clarke scoring the vital goal that gave Don Revie's Leeds the Cup on the away goals rule. Leeds were becoming something of a draw specialist – having a goalless draw at home in the Second Leg of the Semi-Final (against Liverpool; Billy Bremner scored the goal that took them through at Anfield) meant that they became **the ONLY team to win a knockout competition without actually winning any of their last three games**.

THE LAST
INTERNATIONAL
MATCH FOR PELÉ

Brazil v Yugoslavia at Maracana Stadium, Rio de Janeiro, Brazil, Sunday 18 July 1971

Pelé's 92nd and last international was a home game against Yugoslavia in a career that began on 7 July 1957 against Argentina (Brazil lost that game 2-1). The following year he embarked on the first of four World Cup tournaments (1958, 1962, 1966 and 1970) and became the youngest goal scorer (against Wales in the Quarter-Final) and the youngest hat-trick scorer (against France in the Semi-Final). On 19 June 1958 Pelé became the youngest player to play in a World Cup Final at 17 years and 249 days. He scored two goals when Brazil beat Sweden 5-2. In the 1970 Final in which Brazil beat Italy 4-1, defender Tarcisio Burgnich marked Pelé. He said, 'I told myself before the game, he's made of skin and bones just like everyone else – but I was wrong.' After retiring from his club Santos and Brazil, Pelé played for the New York Cosmos for two years. (See 2005, page 214).

THE FIRST
BRITISH CLUB TO SIGN PLAYERS FROM
BEHIND THE IRON CURTAIN
HAMILTON ACADEMICAL, 1971–1972

In 1971 Hamilton Academical were struggling at the bottom of the Scottish Division Two. Their chairman was the Polish electrical shop owner Jan Stepek and he arranged for white goods to be shipped to his homeland. In return the Poles allowed three internationals to join Accies – forward Alfie Olek, midfielder Roman Strazalkowski and goalkeeper Witold Szygula. Thanks to bureaucratic red tape, the arrival of the players was delayed for six months. Strazalkowski had captained Poland in a match against Brazil. Alan Dick, Accies secretary at the time, remembered:

'It was a remarkable deal. Jan Stepek sent fridge freezers and other mechanical appliances to Poland, and in return their authorities allowed three of their top players to come to Hamilton. They were full-time players, and clearly too good for us, which is why they didn't stay longer than a few months, but were paid only a very basic wage of under £200 [between them] per week.'

THE FIRST
EUROPEAN FINAL
BETWEEN ENGLISH TEAMS
TOTTENHAM HOTSPUR V WOLVERHAMPTON WANDERERS, UEFA CUP FINAL AT MOLINEUX GROUNDS, WOLVERHAMPTON, STAFFORDSHIRE, ENGLAND, WEDNESDAY 3 MAY 1972 (FIRST LEG); AT WHITE HART LANE, 748 HIGH ROAD, TOTTENHAM, LONDON, ENGLAND, WEDNESDAY 17 MAY 1972 (SECOND LEG)

The first all-English final was the 14th Fairs/first Uefa Cup Final, a trophy that had been won by English clubs on 11 September 1968 (Leeds

United), 11 June 1969 (Newcastle United), 28 April 1970 (Arsenal) and 3 June 1971 (Leeds United). Spurs won the First Leg at Molineux 2-1 with both Lilywhite goals coming from Martin Chivers (in the 57th and 87th minutes). Captain Jim McCalliog scored for Wolves in the 72nd minute to level the scores. Needing to win by two clear goals or score at least three at White Hart Lane, the task was beyond Wolves and they managed just a one-all draw with goals from Alan Mullery (Spurs) and David Wagstaffe (Wolves). Spurs having won the European Cup Winners' Cup in 1963, Liverpool won the Uefa Cup in 1973 to keep the run of wins by English clubs, although Spurs let the side down in 1974 losing to Feyenoord 4-2 on aggregate. In 1984 Spurs became **the FIRST team to win the Uefa Cup on a penalty shoot-out** when they beat Anderlecht 4-3 after the aggregate score was 2-2. Oddly, when Tottenham's great rivals Arsenal beat Anderlecht to win what was then the Fairs Cup in 1970, they also won 4-3.

WITH THIS VICTORY, SPURS ALSO BECAME:
The FIRST British team to win two major European trophies, having previously won the European Cup Winners' Cup in 1963

THE FIRST
CLUB BANNED FROM
DEFENDING A EUROPEAN TROPHY
RANGERS V MOSCOW DYNAMO, EUROPEAN CUP WINNERS' CUP FINAL
AT CAMP NOU, BARCELONA, SPAIN, WEDNESDAY 24 MAY 1972

At their third attempt in 1972 Rangers finally won the European Cup Winners' Cup, beating Moscow Dynamo 3-2 in Spain. They had previously lost in 1961 to Florence in the first Final and in 1967 to Bayern Munich. When the referee blew the whistle to signal a Rangers victory their rather excitable fans stormed onto the pitch, with the result that the Glaswegians had to be presented with the trophy in their dressing room. Uefa was not impressed and banned Rangers from defending the trophy in the next season. Rangers were lucky to be in the competition at all. On 20 October 1971 they beat Sporting Lisbon at home 3-2 in the

First Leg of the Second Round, but lost the Second Leg 4-3, thus winning on the away goals rule. However, Peter van Ravens, the referee of the Second Leg, didn't quite understand the nuance of the away goal rules and thinking that the match had been tied ordered a penalty shoot-out, which Sporting Lisbon won 2-0. Rangers protested to Uefa, who upheld their complaint.

THERE WERE ALSO TWO ONLYS IN THIS MATCH:
The ONLY team to win a European trophy having been knocked out of the competition • The ONLY European club trophy presented in the winners' dressing room

THE LAST
INTERNATIONAL MATCH
FOR GORDON BANKS
SCOTLAND V ENGLAND AT HAMPDEN PARK, MOUNT FLORIDA, GLASGOW, LANARKSHIRE, SCOTLAND, SATURDAY 27 MAY 1972

Gordon 'Banks of England' played his 73rd and last game for the national team in a 1-0 win against the auld enemy at Hampden Park. Banks was 34 and as a goalkeeper could expect a few more years at the top, but on 22 October 1972 as he was driving home he lost control of his car and in the accident was robbed of the sight in his right eye. He attempted to play on, but the lack of binocular vision prevented him from succeeding and he retired in 1978.

BANKS'S PRETENDER
In 1967, just one year after he had won a World Cup winner's medal with England, Gordon Banks was sold by Leicester City to Stoke City because a young player refused to sign professional terms unless he was guaranteed first team football. The youngster's name was Peter Shilton. In 1974 when Banks left Stoke, the man signed to replace him between the sticks was Peter Shilton.

THE ONLY

TV PRESENTER TO BECOME A
LINESMAN

JIMMY HILL, ARSENAL V LIVERPOOL AT ARSENAL STADIUM, AVENELL ROAD, HIGHBURY, LONDON, ENGLAND, SATURDAY 16 SEPTEMBER 1972

Arsenal were playing host to Liverpool when linesman Dennis Drewitt was injured. TV presenter Jimmy Hill who was a qualified referee came down from the commentary box and ran the line for the rest of the match, which ended goalless.

THE LAST

MATCH BOBBY CHARLTON
PLAYED FOR MANCHESTER UNITED

CHELSEA V MANCHESTER UNITED AT STAMFORD BRIDGE, FULHAM ROAD, FULHAM, LONDON, ENGLAND, SATURDAY 28 APRIL 1973

Having survived the Munich air crash that killed eight of his teammates in 1958, Bobby Charlton became a legend at Manchester United being appointed club captain in 1966, the year he was named European Footballer of the Year. By 1973, however, the good times were over and the team were no longer competing for trophies. Added to this Charlton was not even on speaking terms with some of his teammates, including Denis Law and George Best who refused to play in Charlton's testimonial against Celtic. Charlton left United at the end of the 1972–1973 season, having scored 249 goals and set a club record of 758 appearances (the record was finally broken by Ryan Giggs in 2008). Charlton's last game was away to Chelsea and before the game the Chelsea chairman presented Charlton with a commemorative cigarette case. Sadly for Charlton, the result went Chelsea's way – they won 1-0.

THE LAST

FA CUP FINAL
WON BY A TEAM
WITHOUT ANY INTERNATIONAL PLAYERS

SUNDERLAND V LEEDS UNITED AT WEMBLEY STADIUM, MIDDLESEX,
ENGLAND, 3 PM SATURDAY 5 MAY 1973

Bob Stokoe's Sunderland were the last team to win the FA Cup without a single international player in their ranks. In fact, only one of their players had even been to Wembley (which was celebrating its 50th birthday) before and that was defender Richie Pitt, who had once been to the ground to watch an England schoolboys' international. Irrespective of that, they managed to overcome Leeds, the Cup holders, through a goal from Ian Porterfield on 31 minutes. Bobby Kerr, who at just over 5 ft 4 in (1.62 m) was the smallest FA Cup-winning captain, lifted the Cup.

SUNDERLAND WERE ALSO:
The LAST FA Cup winners to play with an orange ball

THE LAST

WATNEY CUP FINAL
Stoke City v Hull City at Victoria Ground, Stoke-on-Trent,
Staffordshire, England, Saturday 18 August 1973

The Watney Cup — or to give it its official name The Watney Mann Invitation Cup — lasted just four years (1970–1973) and was held before the start of the season. Two teams took part from each of the four divisions and they were selected from the highest scorers in each division who had not been promoted or qualified to play in Europe. There was a simple knockout with no replays and the Final was, unusually, held at the home of one of the finalists.

THE FIRST

WALES PLAYER SENT OFF IN AN
INTERNATIONAL

TREVOR HOCKEY, WALES V POLAND AT CHORZÓW, KATOWICE, POLAND, WEDNESDAY 26 SEPTEMBER 1973

Aston Villa's bearded midfielder Trevor Hockey was the first Welsh international dismissed. His sending-off came during a Group 5 World Cup qualifying match in Poland. Wales lost 3-0. The Poles qualified for the Finals over England and Wales. Hockey died from a heart attack after taking part in a five-a-side tournament in Keighley, Yorkshire on 2 April 1987. He was 43.

THE LAST

INTERNATIONAL MATCH FOR
BOBBY MOORE

ENGLAND V ITALY AT WEMBLEY STADIUM, MIDDLESEX, ENGLAND, WEDNESDAY 14 NOVEMBER 1973

The only England player to lift the World Cup, Bobby Moore won his 108th and last cap in a friendly against Italy at Wembley, which England lost 1-0 thanks to a goal from Fabio Capello. Nine months earlier Moore had won his 100th cap in a 5-0 win over Scotland, becoming the third player to achieve a century of caps for England. Moore died of cancer on 24 February 1993. (See 1966, pages 135 and 136).

THE LAST

MATCH GEORGE BEST
PLAYED FOR MANCHESTER UNITED

QUEENS PARK RANGERS V MANCHESTER UNITED AT LOFTUS ROAD, SOUTH AFRICA ROAD, SHEPHERD'S BUSH, LONDON, ENGLAND, TUESDAY 1 JANUARY 1974

George Best signed professional forms with Manchester United on 22 May 1963 and made his first appearance at Old Trafford aged 17 on 14

September 1963 against West Bromwich Albion in a 1-0 victory before 50,453 spectators. Less than a year later, on 15 April 1964, he made his international debut for Northern Ireland against Wales. Brilliant as he was, Best could not control his demons of gambling, alcoholism and violence towards women. His last of 470 games for Manchester United came in west London on New Year's Day 1974. United lost 3-0. Best, aged just 27, was heavily bearded and overweight. On 3 January he failed to turn up for training and although he arrived the next day manager Tommy Docherty dropped him. Best never played for United again and joined Jewish Guild in South Africa in May, but left after only five games.

His footballing career declined as he joined several teams, but didn't have the discipline to play more than a handful of games before leaving. In 1984 he was jailed for drink driving. Despite undergoing a liver transplant in August 2002, Best continued to drink and died on 25 November 2005. He had a penchant for beautiful blondes and squired, among many others, Miss World Marjorie Wallace (who had him arrested when she alleged that he had stolen her diary), Miss World Mary Stavin, Juliet Mills, Annette Andre, Sinéad Cusack, Lynsey de Paul, Stephanie Sheen, Angie MacDonald Janes (who he made his first wife), Georgie Ellis (the daughter of Ruth Ellis, the last woman hanged for murder in Great Britain) and Alex Pursey (who made a career out of being his second wife and even went on the reality show *I'm A Celebrity... Get Me Out Of Here!*). Both wives wrote autobiographies.

THE FIRST
FA CUP MATCH
PLAYED ON THE SABBATH
CAMBRIDGE UNITED V OLDHAM ATHLETIC AT ABBEY STADIUM, NEWMARKET ROAD, CAMBRIDGE, ENGLAND, 11 AM ON SUNDAY 6 JANUARY 1974

Four Third Round FA Cup ties were played on the first Sunday in 1974. The first to kick off was Cambridge's home tie with Oldham. The match ended in a 2-2 draw and a replay at Oldham two days later finished three-all after extra time. A second replay was held at City Ground, Nottingham on 14 January and Oldham won 2-1. **The FIRST Division One match played on a Sunday** occurred three weeks later when Stoke City beat Chelsea 1-0 at Victoria Ground.

THE LAST

MATCH FOR SIR ALF RAMSEY AS ENGLAND MANAGER

PORTUGAL V ENGLAND AT ESTÁDIO DA LUZ, LISBON, PORTUGAL, WEDNESDAY 3 APRIL 1974

Eight years after winning England its only international trophy Sir Alf Ramsey was ignominiously sacked as manager. In his last match in charge he gave caps to six debutants: Queens Park Rangers' goalkeeper Phil Parkes (his only cap), Stoke City left back Mike Pejic (the first of his four caps), Burnley's midfielder Martin Dobson (the first of five appearances in an England shirt), Sunderland's centre half Dave Watson (the first of his 65 caps), midfielder Stan Bowles, also from QPR (first of five caps) and Trevor Brooking (the first of 47 caps for the West Ham legend). Rather than in glory, the match ended in a damp squib goalless draw.

THE LAST

FA AMATEUR CUP FINAL

BISHOP'S STORTFORD V ILFORD AT WEMBLEY STADIUM, MIDDLESEX, ENGLAND, SATURDAY 20 APRIL 1974

In 1974 the FA abolished amateur status for footballers, insisting that they all be called 'players' irrespective of whether they were paid for turning out. The final Final was contested between Bishop's Stortford from Hertfordshire and Ilford from Essex. In front of more than 30,000 spectators Bishop's Stortford in their centenary season won convincingly 4-1 with goals from Dave Lawrence, Peter Leakey, Dennis Murphy and Martin Smith from the penalty spot.

THE ONLY
ENGLAND PLAYER WHOSE FIRST THREE GAMES WERE
AGAINST SAME OPPOSITION

Kevin Keegan, England v Wales at Ninian Park, Cardiff, Glamorgan, Wales, Wednesday 15 November 1972; England v Wales at Wembley Stadium, Middlesex, England, Sunday 21 January 1973; England v Wales at Ninian Park, Cardiff, Glamorgan, Wales, Saturday 11 May 1974

The be-permed striker made his debut against Wales at Cardiff aged 21 years and 275 days in Group 5 of the World Cup 1974 qualifying rounds and England won 1-0. The game also marked the debut of goalkeeper Ray Clemence. Two months later the two countries met in the second World Cup qualifier and shared two goals. Keegan was then not selected for more than a year, but returned to the team for the Home Championship match at Ninian Park, where he scored his first goal in England's colours.

THE ONLY
EUROPEAN CUP FINAL REPLAY

Atlético Madrid v Bayern Munich at Stade du Heysel, Brussels, Belgium, Friday 17 May 1974

Two days after Atlético Madrid and Bayern Munich had played a 120-minute one-all deadlock the teams met again at the same venue for the only European Cup Final replay. This time there was little doubt as to the victors – Bayern thumped four past the unfortunate Spaniards, two from Gerd Müller and two from Uli Hoeness. The match is also noteworthy because it attracted just 23,009 spectators – the lowest attendance figure for a European Cup Final.

THE FIRST
RED CARD

CARLOS CASZELY, CHILE V WEST GERMANY AT OLYMPIASTADION, WEST BERLIN, WEST GERMANY, 4 PM FRIDAY 14 JUNE 1974

Four years after their introduction at the 1970 World Cup, Chilean forward Carlos Caszely, 23, became the first player to be shown a red card after he kicked West German right back Berti Vogts in the 67th minute. Today, Caszely works as a television presenter.

THE ONLY

MATCH BETWEEN
EAST AND WEST GERMANY

EAST GERMANY V WEST GERMANY AT VOLKSPARKSTADION, HAMBURG, WEST GERMANY, 7.30 PM SATURDAY 22 JUNE 1974

Since the end of the Second World War Germany had been split into two, but the two countries had never met on a football pitch. That changed in the 1974 World Cup when they were both selected for Group A of the tournament. The match was the third game for both teams – East Germany having beaten Australia 2-0 and drawn one-all with Chile, while West Germany beat Chile 1-0 and put three past Australia without conceding a goal. The line-ups were: East Germany – Jürgen Croy, Bernd Bransch (captain), Gerd Kische, Konrad Weise, Siegmar Wätzlich, Reinhard Lauck, Harald Irmscher (replaced in the 65th minute by Erich Hamann), Lothar Kurbjuweit, Jürgen Sparwasser, Hans-Jürgen Kreische and Martin Hoffmann; West Germany – Sepp Maier, Franz Beckenbauer, Berti Vogts, Hans-Georg Schwarzenbeck (replaced in the 68th minute by Horst-Dieter Höttges), Paul Breitner, Uli Hoeness, Bernhard Cullmann, Wolfgang Overath (replaced in the 69th minute by Gunter Netzer), Jürgen Grabowski, Gerd Müller and Heinz Flohe.

This historic match was refereed by Barreto Ruiz of Uruguay and watched by 62,000 spectators. The only goal came in the 78th minute when Sparwasser won the game for East Germany, no doubt to the great pleasure of their Soviet masters. Both teams qualified for the next stage, which was another league tournament. East Germany went into Group I, while West Germany entered Group II. This time West Germany won all three of their matches, while East Germany drew one and lost two (Argentina, and Holland and Brazil respectively). East Germany went home, while West Germany went on to win the competition. (See page 158.)

THE FIRST
PENALTY AWARDED
IN A WORLD CUP FINAL

HOLLAND V WEST GERMANY AT OLYMPIASTADION, MUNICH,
WEST GERMANY, 4 PM SUNDAY 7 JULY 1974

English referee Jack Taylor was about to blow the whistle to start the biggest match of his career when he looked around to make sure that everything was ready. It was then that the eagle-eyed man in black noticed that none of the corner posts had flags on them. When the match finally did kick off, Uli Hoeness fouled Johan Cruyff and Taylor pointed to the spot. Johan Neeskens converted the first penalty in a World Cup Final after two minutes. On 25 minutes Taylor awarded the West Germans a penalty against Holland's Wim Jansen for 'attempting to trip' the West German left midfielder Bernd Hölzenbein and Paul Breitner equalized. Taylor later said:

'The first penalty wasn't difficult to call. All I remember is thinking it was a 100 per cent correct decision. As the ball went on the spot the whole stadium went quiet. Beckenbauer, the German skipper, came to me and said, "Taylor, you're an Englishman." The kick went in and there was complete euphoria. What really does annoy me is the suggestion that I gave [the second penalty] to even things up. It was a trip or an attempted trip and the laws of the game are that's a penalty.'

On 43 minutes Gerd Müller scored West Germany's winning goal.

THIS MATCH ALSO FEATURED A LAST AND AN ONLY: The LAST international goal scored by Gerd Müller, which won the match • The ONLY World Cup Final delayed because there were no corner flags

THE FIRST
CHARITY SHIELD AT WEMBLEY

LEEDS UNITED V LIVERPOOL AT WEMBLEY STADIUM, MIDDLESEX,
ENGLAND, SATURDAY 10 AUGUST 1974

Brian Clough's Leeds United (Division One champions) and Bob Paisley's Liverpool (FA Cup winners) met for the first Charity Shield played at

Wembley and broadcast live. It was the first game in charge for both managers, although former boss Bill Shankly led out the Reds. The match ended 1-1 with Phil Boersma scoring for Liverpool after 20 minutes before Trevor Cherry equalized for Leeds with 70 minutes on the clock. Both sides scored their first five penalties before Leeds goalie David Harvey missed from the spot, hitting the ball over the bar. Ian Callaghan didn't miss for Liverpool, who won 6-5. It was also remarkable for the first double sending-off at Wembley, Leeds United's Billy Bremner and Liverpool's Kevin Keegan being dismissed for fighting and both ripping off their shirts in disgust as they left the pitch. For their petulant behaviour both were fined £500 and suspended for 11 games. Liverpool's Tommy Smith, no slouch in the hard man's department himself, recalled:

'We went at each other hammer and tongs. Nobody was going to shy away, and there was no complaining or whining on the field that day. As for the sendings-off, Leeds had been getting at Kevin all day, Johnny Giles in particular. It was at a corner, and Giles came up behind Keegan and whacked him. Kevin whirled round, but Giles had disappeared and Billy was the nearest Leeds player, so Kevin went for him. Okay, so Billy ended up throwing punches too, but it should have been Giles who got Kevin's attention.'

Brian Clough, who spent just 44 days at Elland Road, had a different memory:

'Billy Bremner's behaviour was scandalous... [He] seemed intent on making Kevin Keegan's afternoon an absolute misery. He kicked him just about everywhere... until it became only a matter of time before a confrontation exploded. There is only so much any man can take. Eventually, inevitably, Keegan snapped – and they were both sent off, Keegan whipping off his shirt and flinging it to the ground as he went. It was a stupid gesture, but I could understand the man's anger and frustration. It was the action of a player who felt he had been wronged, not only by an opponent but by a referee who had failed to stamp out intimidation before it reached the stage of retaliation... I told Bremner afterwards that he had been responsible for the confrontation. He should have been made to pay compensation for the lengthy period Keegan was suspended.'

OTHER FIRSTS IN THIS MATCH: The FIRST double sending-off at Wembley • The FIRST Charity Shield broadcast live • The FIRST major domestic trophy decided by penalties

THE ONLY
2-2 DRAW IN THE FOOTBALL LEAGUE IN WHICH
TWO PLAYERS SCORED FOR BOTH TEAMS
TOTTENHAM HOTSPUR V BURNLEY AT TURF MOOR, BURNLEY, LANCASHIRE, ENGLAND, SATURDAY 5 OCTOBER 1974

North Londoners Spurs travelled north to Burnley in the autumn of 1974 and by half-time found that they were two goals adrift. To make matters worse Spurs players John Pratt and Mike England both scored own goals. Spurs manager Bill Nicholson obviously had some encouraging words for his team because by the time the referee blew for time on 90 minutes the score was 2-2 and the two second-half goals were also scored by John Pratt and Mike England.

THE LAST
FA CUP WINNERS WITH
11 ENGLISH PLAYERS
West Ham United v Fulham at Wembley Stadium, Middlesex, England, Saturday 3 May 1975

West Ham boss John Lyall took a team chockfull of Englishmen to Wembley for the 1975 Final to face west Londoners Fulham. Fulham chief Alec Stock also had an abundance of Englishmen in his side – ten – the exception being Irish-born number eight Jimmy Conway. On the Fulham side in the heart of defence was former Hammers hero Bobby Moore and they had another former England captain in their ranks in the shape of Alan Mullery. The match was played in such a sporting atmosphere that neither trainer had occasion to set foot on the hallowed Wembley turf.

THIS MATCH WAS ALSO: The ONLY FA Cup Final appearance by Fulham

THE ONLY
PLAYER TO DISLOCATE HIS JAW
SHOUTING AT HIS TEAMMATES

Alex Stepney, Manchester United v Birmingham City at St Andrews, Birmingham, England, Tuesday 19 August 1975

Manchester United's vociferous goalkeeper Alex Stepney could never be accused of not giving his all. In United's match with Birmingham City at the start of the 1975–1976 season he was taken to hospital after he dislocated his jaw shouting at his defenders. It seemed to work – United won 2-0, with Sammy McIlroy netting both goals.

THE ONLY
MAN TO PLAY
FIRST CLASS FOOTBALL AND FIRST CLASS CRICKET
ON THE SAME DAY

CHRIS BALDERSTONE, DONCASTER ROVERS V BRENTFORD AT BELLE VUE GROUND, DONCASTER, SOUTH YORKSHIRE, ENGLAND; LEICESTERSHIRE V DERBYSHIRE AT QUEEN'S PARK, CHESTERFIELD, ENGLAND, MONDAY 15 SEPTEMBER 1975

Chris Balderstone became the only man to play First Class cricket and first class football on the same day in the autumn of 1975. He played for Leicestershire against Derbyshire at Queen's Park, Chesterfield and was on 51 when bad light stopped play. That evening he turned out in midfield for Doncaster Rovers in a 1-1 draw against Brentford in Division Four. When that match had finished he played darts for Doncaster Rovers players' team against a supporters' team in the Rovers supporters' club. The following day he resumed his innings and was finally run out for 116. He died aged 59 on 6 March 2000.

THE LAST

INTER-LEAGUE MATCH

SCOTTISH LEAGUE V FOOTBALL LEAGUE AT HAMPDEN PARK,
MOUNT FLORIDA, GLASGOW, LANARKSHIRE, SCOTLAND,
WEDNESDAY 17 MARCH 1976

Beginning at Sheffield on 20 April 1891, Inter-League matches were contested between the Football League and their counterparts the Scottish League, Irish League, League of Ireland and Welsh League, in 1952–1953 the Danish League and in 1967 the Belgian League. **The FIRST Inter-League match** was between the Football League and the Alliance (Southern) League, with **the FIRST Football League against the Scottish League** ending in a 2-2 draw on 11 April 1892 at Pike's Lane, Bolton.

England manager Walter Winterbottom was given charge of the Football League team in the 1950s and managed to persuade the Football Association to select players for Inter-League matches rather than England as their way of 'reward[ing] a player for being a good sportsman'. The rules stated that players could represent the nation where they played, but not that country if they had been born elsewhere, so Joe Baker of Hibernian was allowed to play for the Scottish League, but played internationally for England, having been born at Liverpool. His brother Gerry who played for St Mirren also played for the Scottish League, but played internationally for Canada where he was born. German Bert Trautmann was **the ONLY foreigner to play for the Football League**, while Scot Denis Law (Turin) and Welshman John Charles (Juventus) played for the Italian League against the Scottish League at Hampden Park on 1 November 1961 when the Italians won 3-2.

Just 8,874 watched the last Inter-League match, down from an all-time high of 90,987 who had watched a previous encounter between the two teams. The Scottish League team consisted of Jim Stewart (Kilmarnock), Andy Rolland (Dundee United), Joe Wark (Motherwell), Tom Forsyth (Rangers), Colin Jackson (Rangers), Willie Miller (Aberdeen), Arthur Duncan (Hibernian), Des Bremner (Hibernian), David Craig (Partick Thistle), John McDonald (Rangers) and Bobby McKean (Rangers). Representing the Football League were Peter Shilton (Stoke City), Trevor Cherry (Leeds United), Mick Doyle (Manchester City), Roy McFarland

(Derby County), Colin Todd (Derby County), Ray Wilkins (Chelsea), Mick Channon (Southampton), Jimmy Greenhoff (Stoke City), Tony Currie (Sheffield United) and Dennis Tueart (Manchester City). The match ended in a 1-0 victory for the Football League thanks to a Trevor Cherry goal and then the competition died for lack of interest and pressure of fixtures.

THE FIRST
RED CARD
IN THE FOOTBALL LEAGUE
DAVID WAGSTAFFE, BLACKBURN ROVERS V ORIENT AT LEYTON STADIUM, BRISBANE ROAD, LONDON, ENGLAND, SATURDAY 2 OCTOBER 1976

Six years after their first use in the World Cup, red cards were introduced in English football. David Wagstaffe has the dubious honour of being the first player in the Football League to be shown a red card when he was dismissed in Blackburn's away game against Orient in Division Two.

THE FIRST
PLAYER TO CAPTAIN WINNING TEAMS
IN THE FA CUP AND THE SCOTTISH FA CUP
MARTIN BUCHAN, ABERDEEN V CELTIC AT HAMPDEN PARK, MOUNT FLORIDA, GLASGOW, LANARKSHIRE, SCOTLAND, SATURDAY 11 APRIL 1970; MANCHESTER UNITED V LIVERPOOL AT WEMBLEY STADIUM, MIDDLESEX, ENGLAND, 3 PM SATURDAY 21 MAY 1977

Martin Buchan joined Aberdeen in 1966 and played 136 times for the Dons, captaining them to their second victory in the Scottish FA Cup. They beat Celtic 3-1. On 29 February 1972 Frank O'Farrell signed him for Manchester United for £120,000 – then the club's most expensive signing. Buchan went on to become a key component of new manager Tommy Docherty's side after O'Farrell's sacking. Buchan was in the team that lost to Southampton in 1976, but came back the following season to beat the more powerful Liverpool. All three goals – Jimmy Case for Liverpool and Stuart Pearson and Jimmy Greenhoff for Manchester United – came in a five-minute period early in the second half. The victory prevented Liverpool from achieving a treble of League Championship, FA Cup and European Cup.

INTERNATIONAL MATCH FOR
JOHAN CRUYFF

HOLLAND V BELGIUM AT AMSTERDAM, HOLLAND, WEDNESDAY 26 OCTOBER 1977

The Dutch football master was **the FIRST man to win the European Player of the Year Award three times**, triumphing in 1971, 1973 and 1974. He made his international debut on 7 September 1966 against Hungary and played 48 times for Holland, scoring 33 goals. In his second match (a friendly against Czechoslovakia on 6 November 1966) he became **the FIRST Dutch international player to be sent off** and received a year's suspension. He was captain of the losing Dutch side in the 1974 World Cup Final and was booked for back-chatting referee Jack Taylor. He retired after helping Holland qualify for the 1978 World Cup when someone tried to kidnap his family in Barcelona the year before. He said, 'To play a World Cup you have to be 200 per cent; there are moments when there are other values in life.' (See 1989, page 184).

THE FIRST
CLUB TO WEAR A
SPONSOR'S NAME ON THEIR SHIRTS
DERBY COUNTY, ENGLAND, 1977–1978

In the summer of 1978 Derby County, managed by Tommy Docherty, were the first Football League club to sign a sponsorship deal for their shirts. In the pre-season publicity pictures the players posed with 'Saab' in red lettering on their shirts, but the Football League refused to allow sponsorship, so the club never wore them in a competitive match. In 1979 the League relented and Liverpool became **the First English club to play in sponsored (by Hitachi) shirts**. In 1977–1978 Hibernian were **the First senior club in Britain to sport sponsored shirts**.

THE ONLY
BRITISH PLAYER TO FAIL A WORLD CUP DRUGS TEST
WILLIE JOHNSTON, SCOTLAND, SATURDAY 3 JUNE 1978

On 3 June 1978 Scotland lost 3-1 to Peru at Estadio Chateau Carreras, Cordoba, Argentina in their first World Cup match of the tournament. Afterwards, as was commonplace, Scotland's Willie Johnston in his 21st international appearance over 13 years was randomly picked for a mandatory drugs test. The West Bromwich Albion winger failed the test and was sent home in disgrace and banned for life by the Scottish Football Association. Johnston claimed that he was taking nothing stronger than Reactivan to treat a cold, but the SFA would not allow a second test to establish his innocence or guilt. His career at West Brom fizzled out and he later ran a pub in Kirkaldy, Fife. Johnston said:

'I was hung out to dry by the Scottish FA. I would have liked them to appeal against it and arrange for me to have a second test, but they didn't and they told me to pack my bags and leave. I just wanted to play at a World Cup – it was my ambition. I played one game and got sent home.'

THE FIRST
PLAYER SOLD FOR A £1 MILLION TRANSFER
Trevor Francis, Birmingham City to Nottingham Forest, England, Friday 9 February 1979

Brian Clough paid a cool million to bring 24-year-old striker Trevor Francis to the City Ground. On the day of the announcement Clough had arranged a squash match and turned up for the press conference in his gym kit carrying a squash racquet. In fact, Clough paid Birmingham City £975,000 for Francis. However, with the necessary taxes and Francis's percentage, the final sum was £1,180,000.

THE ONLY
PLAYER TO APPEAR IN DIFFERENT
FA CUP FINAL-WINNING TEAMS
IN SUCCESSIVE SEASONS

BRIAN TALBOT, IPSWICH TOWN V ARSENAL AT WEMBLEY STADIUM, MIDDLESEX, ENGLAND, SATURDAY 6 MAY 1978; ARSENAL V MANCHESTER UNITED AT WEMBLEY STADIUM, MIDDLESEX, ENGLAND, SATURDAY 12 MAY 1979

After winning an FA Cup winner's medal with the Tractor Boys in 1978, Talbot subsequently signed for Arsenal for £450,000 in January 1979. The following year he was back at Wembley in the yellow shirt of Arsenal, where he scored Arsenal's first goal when they beat Manchester United in a hotly fought contest.

THE LAST
INTERNATIONAL MATCH
FOR SEPP MAIER

ICELAND V WEST GERMANY AT REYKJAVIK, ICELAND, SATURDAY 26 MAY 1979

Born in 1944, Josef 'Sepp' Maier was the leading German goalkeeper in the 1970s representing his country 95 times – the first against Ireland at Dublin on 4 May 1966. Despite his reputation as a fine goalie, he let in 80 goals and kept a clean sheet on just 38 occasions, although not on the last occasion when he let one in as West Germany won 3-1. His career came to an end when he was involved in a car crash after drinking too much. Recovered from life-threatening injuries, he became goalkeeping coach to Bayern Munich, his old club, and the German national side, but was sacked in October 2004 by manager Jürgen Klinsmann for criticizing the selection of Arsenal's Jens Lehmann as national goalkeeper over Bayern Munich's Oliver Kahn. Maier retired from Bayern in 2008.

THE FIRST

SENIOR ALL-SEATER STADIUM
IN GREAT BRITAIN

Pittodrie, Aberdeen, Scotland, Sunday 1 July 1979

Pittodrie was **the FIRST football ground to have dug-outs** (installed in the 1920s) and in the summer of 1979 became the first stadium in Britain that was all-seater. **The FIRST all-seater stadium in England** was Portman Road, the home of Ipswich Town.

THE ONLY

PLAYER SENT OFF
WHILE TAKING A PENALTY

DIXIE MCNEILL, WREXHAM V CHARLTON ATHLETIC AT THE RACECOURSE GROUND, MOLD ROAD, WREXHAM, WALES, SATURDAY 19 JANUARY 1980

With the score at two apiece in the Division Two match between Wrexham and Charlton the Robins were awarded a penalty. Dixie McNeill stood up to take it, but was twice put off by banter from the Addicks players. Frustrated, he kicked the ball into the crowd and was promptly sent off by the referee. As McNeill fumed in his early bath, Mick Vinter took the kick and scored to give Wrexham a 3-2 victory. The season also saw Charlton relegated to Division Three.

THE FIRST
BRITISH CLUB TO BEAT JUVENTUS IN TURIN
ARSENAL V JUVENTUS AT STADIO COMMUNALE, TURIN, ITALY, WEDNESDAY 23 APRIL 1980

Having beaten Manchester United in the FA Cup Final the previous May, Arsenal gained entrance to the European Cup Winners' Cup. Terry Neill's men progressed to the Semi-Final where they were drawn against Italian giants Juventus. Few neutrals gave the Gunners a chance in the Second Leg in Turin before 66,386 fans (Arsenal drew the First Leg at Highbury 1-1), but they reckoned without a curly-headed youngster called Paul Vaessen. With 15 minutes remaining on the clock Terry Neill pulled off the tired David Price and replaced him with Vaessen. With two minutes to go he scored the most important goal of his career. Graham Rix crossed and Vaessen jumped to head home. It was the first time any British team had beaten Juventus at the Italian club's home ground.

Further glory was not to come Vaessen's way. Injury forced him to retire from the game in the summer of 1983, aged just 21. He had scored nine goals in 39 games for Arsenal. The club did little for the ex-player after his retirement and he worked in a number of menial jobs, but unable to cope he became a heroin addict. An attempt to train as a physiotherapist ended in failure and on 8 August 2001 he was found dead in his bathroom in Henbury, Bristol with a large amount of drugs in his bloodstream. He was 39.

THE ONLY
TEAM IN THE 20TH CENTURY TO REACH THREE SUCCESSIVE FA CUP FINALS
ARSENAL V IPSWICH TOWN AT WEMBLEY STADIUM, MIDDLESEX ENGLAND, SATURDAY 6 MAY 1978; V MANCHESTER UNITED AT WEMBLEY STADIUM, MIDDLESEX, ENGLAND, SATURDAY 12 MAY 1979; V WEST HAM UNITED AT WEMBLEY STADIUM, MIDDLESEX, ENGLAND, SATURDAY 10 MAY 1980

Under the managership of former player Terry Neill, Arsenal were the only team in the 20th century to reach three successive FA Cup Finals. Six years to the day after they lost 1-0 to Leeds United in the 1972 FA Cup Final, Arsenal returned to Wembley to meet Ipswich Town. Around 100,000 people saw Paul Mariner and George Burley almost score for the Tractor Boys, but the woodwork and Pat Jennings saved Arsenal. After 76 minutes Ipswich attacked and Willie Young miss-hit his clearance, the ball landing at the feet of Roger Osborne, who belted it past Jennings to take the Cup by the now familiar score line of 1-0. Arsenal's Pat Rice was the only survivor from the 1972 Cup Final.

A year later the Gunners were back at the twin towers and their opponents were Manchester United in their third Final in four years. Arsenal were determined to make up for their defeat the year before. There were 15 internationals on the pitch, but the game was hardly chockfull of skill and finesse. Arsenal had despatched assistant manager Wilf Dixon and ex-Gunner George Male to compile a dossier to find United's weaknesses. They worked out that the United defence had a tendency to bunch together and did not defend the far post during crosses. Brian Talbot, who had joined from Ipswich Town for £450,000, opened Arsenal's account from a cross by David Price after a run by Liam Brady. In the Arsenal goal, Jennings was forced into making some good saves to keep the score 1-0. On 43 minutes Liam Brady crossed and Frank Stapleton headed goal number two for Arsenal.

Half-time came and went, and Arsenal seemed to be cruising to an easy win. Then Terry Neill made what is still to some a surprising substitution – he pulled off midfielder David Price and sent on defender Steve Walford. The decision upset the balance of the Arsenal side and suddenly Manchester United sniffed a chance. From a free kick Joe Jordan pulled the ball across Arsenal's goal for Gordon McQueen to score and then two minutes later Sammy McIlroy made it 2-2. It seemed that extra time would be needed as with the 1971 game. Liam Brady said, 'When United pulled level I was dreading extra time because I was knackered and our substitute was already on.' He needn't have worried – he and Arsenal had other ideas: Brady spotted Graham Rix on the left side of the pitch and passed to him, then Rix took off and crossed the ball. Gary Bailey in goal for United misjudged the cross and Alan Sunderland managed to connect with it with enough force to send it over the goal line and give Arsenal a last-minute victory.

GUNNERS' SILVERWARE

Having been the only team to reach three consecutive FA Cup Finals in the 20th century, Arsenal became the FIRST team to repeat the feat in the 21st century when they played in the 2001, 2002 and 2003 Finals. They had more success in the latter Finals, winning two of the three compared to one of the three in the previous century.

In 1980 it was three years and three FA Cup Finals, and Arsenal looked as if they were making Wembley a second home. However, it was again to end in victory for the underdogs. Before 100,000 fans Arsenal faced Division Two West Ham United, who won 1-0.

THE FIRST

EUROPEAN CLUB FINAL DECIDED ON PENALTIES

ARSENAL V VALENCIA, EUROPEAN CUP WINNERS' CUP FINAL AT STADE DU HEYSEL, BRUSSELS, BELGIUM, WEDNESDAY 14 MAY 1980

Four days after they lost to West Ham in the FA Cup Final Arsenal played in another Cup Final. Having seen off the mighty Juventus (see 1980, page 168), Arsenal met the Spaniards from Valencia and were favourites to win as they had been against West Ham. Arsenal centre half David O'Leary didn't train in the run-up to the Final because of a thigh strain and played dosed up on painkillers. With the teams tied at 0-0 after 90 minutes of normal play and 30 minutes of extra time, a European club trophy was decided for the first time on a penalty shoot-out. Mario Kempes (the only non-Spaniard in Valencia's side), described by *The Times* reporter as having 'flowing feminine locks', took the first shot, but Pat Jennings saved his effort. Then Liam Brady stepped up to take the first penalty for Arsenal and promptly missed. All the Valencia players put the ball past Jennings and for Arsenal Frank Stapleton, Alan Sunderland, Brian Talbot and John Hollins all scored. Then Arsenal's curly-headed number 11 Graham Rix stepped up and missed, his shot being saved by keeper Carlos Santiago Pereira. The trophy went home with the Spaniards.

—•••—

THE ONLY
TEAM TO HAVE WON
THE EUROPEAN CUP MORE OFTEN
THAN THEIR DOMESTIC CHAMPIONSHIP

Nottingham Forest, Division One Championship 1978; European Cup Finals, v Malmö of Sweden at Olympiastadion, Munich, West Germany, Wednesday 30 May 1979; v Hamburg SV of West Germany at Santiago Bernabéu Stadium, Madrid, Spain, Wednesday 28 May 1980

Brian Clough's Nottingham Forest, **the ONLY League club not to be a limited company**, won their only League title to date in 1977–1978, their first season in the top division for five years. The following season was their first in the European Cup and they beat the Swedes of Malmö by a single goal headed into the net by million pound striker Trevor Francis. The following season they became the seventh team to retain the trophy when they beat Hamburg SV, again by a single goal that went in off the post, scored by John Robertson in the 21st minute. Clough said, 'The odds were stacked against us... It was one of the best 90 minutes we have ever had, absolutely marvellous.'

—•••—

THE ONLY
ABANDONED HOME CHAMPIONSHIPS
1980–1981

The annual tournament between England, Northern Ireland, Scotland and Wales was abandoned for the only time because of the Troubles in Ulster. Fearful for their safety (several members of the IRA were staging hunger strikes at the time at Long Kesh Prison), England and Wales refused to travel to Belfast and the competition was declared void. (See 1884, page 33 and 1983–1984, page 179.)

THE ONLY
BRITISH MANAGER OF THREE
EUROPEAN CUP-WINNING SIDES

BOB PAISLEY, LIVERPOOL V BORUSSIA MÖNCHENGLADBACH AT STADIO
OLIMPICO, ROME, ITALY, WEDNESDAY 25 MAY 1977; V BRUGE AT WEMBLEY
STADIUM, MIDDLESEX, ENGLAND, WEDNESDAY 10 MAY 1978; V REAL
MADRID AT PARC DES PRINCES, PARIS, FRANCE, WEDNESDAY 27 MAY 1981

Having taken over from Bill Shankly on 26 July 1974, in his nine years in
charge Bob Paisley (1919–1996) led Liverpool to six League titles, three
European Cups, one Uefa Cup, one Uefa Super Cup, three League Cups
and five Charity Shields. As a player Paisley made more than
250 appearances for Liverpool before retiring in 1954. He was named
Manager of the Year six times. (See 1983, page 176)

THE FIRST
LEAGUE CLUB TO INSTALL A
SYNTHETIC PITCH

QUEEN PARK RANGERS AT LOFTUS ROAD, SOUTH AFRICA ROAD,
SHEPHERD'S BUSH, LONDON, ENGLAND, 1981

Following the use of Astroturf in American sporting arenas, in the summer
of 1981 Queens Park Rangers, not long after the appointment of Terry
Venables as manager, dug up the grass at Loftus Road and put down a
synthetic pitch of Omniturf instead. Queens Park Rangers then proceeded
to lose their first match on the new surface – 2-1 to Luton Town. In April
1988 the club reinstated grass on the pitch.

THE FIRST

THREE POINTS FOR A WIN

1981–1982

Having awarded two points for a win since the Football League's inception in 1888 it finally gave in to pressure, and in a bid to encourage more goals and attacking, football changed the points system to three for a win.

THE FIRST

PAID DIRECTOR OF AN ENGLISH CLUB

MALCOLM MACDONALD, FULHAM, CRAVEN COTTAGE, STEVENAGE ROAD, LONDON, ENGLAND, THURSDAY 19 NOVEMBER 1981

The former Newcastle United, Arsenal and England centre forward became the manager of Fulham in 1980 after his premature retirement following a knee injury while playing for the Gunners against Rotherham United in the Second Round of the League Cup on 29 August 1978 in a match that Arsenal lost 3-1. In the 1981–1982 season, which saw Fulham promoted from Division Three to Division Two, Supermac became the first paid director of an English football team. He recalls:

'The appointment was made on the day notification was received at the club that the FA had changed the rules that were now to allow professional – paid – directors. Therefore, I became the first professional director in football. There was much west London rivalry in just about everything between the three chairmen, Ken Bates (Chelsea), Jim Gregory (QPR) and Ernie Clay (Fulham). A few days later Terry Venables was appointed to a similar position or given the title, however you wish to view it, at QPR. In my case it was more of a symbolic gesture by Ernie Clay, who prided himself on being a destroyer of institutionalism and a champion of change. He was a backer and adviser to George Eastham who took Newcastle United to court in 1963 to abolish the maximum wage. He was a right-hand man to Eric Miller who, when chairman of Fulham FC in the mid- to late 1970s, signed the likes of Bobby Moore, George Best, Rodney Marsh and Alan Mullery. My title changed from manager to Director Manager. Make of that what

you will. The pay didn't really change, as he was a chairman who disliked contracts intensely. He would say if you don't like it there is always someone who will. Albeit, he rewarded improvement and success reasonably well.'

He left Craven Cottage in April 1984 and now presents a highly successful radio show.

THE ONLY

FOOTBALL LEAGUE TEAM TO LOSE AT HOME WHILE PLAYING AWAY

OLDHAM ATHLETIC V BLACKBURN ROVERS AT EWOOD PARK, BLACKBURN, LANCASHIRE, ENGLAND, BOXING DAY SATURDAY 26 DECEMBER 1981

When the fixture list for 1981–1982 was drawn up Blackburn were scheduled to play Oldham at Boundary Park, Oldham. However, the Oldham pitch was declared unfit for play and the fixture was changed to Blackburn's ground at Ewood Park, a near 30-mile journey north on the M66. Blackburn Rovers won the match 3-0, but the Football League recorded the result as a home defeat for Oldham, which broke their unbeaten home record for the season to date. On 9 April 1982 the Latics went to Ewood Park for the second time that season and their first 'away' fixture there, and came away with a point from a goalless draw.

THE ONLY

FOOTBALL LEAGUE MATCH IN WHICH FOUR BALLS WERE USED

LEICESTER CITY V FULHAM AT CITY STADIUM, FILBERT STREET, LEICESTER, LEICESTERSHIRE, ENGLAND, SATURDAY 4 DECEMBER 1982

The Second Division tie between the two clubs looked like any other when it kicked off on a cold winter's day. Then the excitement started. A ball was kicked over the stand and disappeared. A new ball was found, but City players complained that it was underinflated and so a third ball was thrown onto the pitch. This time the referee didn't find it to be of acceptable quality and so he asked for a fourth ball, with which the game continued. Leicester won the game 2-0.

THE ONLY
FOOTBALLER MURDERED
BY THE STASI

Lutz Eigendorf, Braunschweig, West Germany, Monday 7 March 1983

East German international Lutz Eigendorf played for Berliner FC Dynamo, but on 21 March 1979, the day after a friendly between 1. FC Kaiserslautern and Berliner FC Dynamo at Giessen, the dark-haired 22-year-old midfielder defected to the West, hoping to play for 1. FC Kaiserslautern. Without embracing the spirit of his bravery, Uefa promptly banned Eigendorf for playing for a year. Berliner FC Dynamo were 'helped' by the Stasi, East Germany's state police, who ensured that the team had the pick of the best players and often fixed results in their favour. In the West Eigendorf was, as it turned out foolishly, highly critical of the East German state. Eigendorf's wife, Gabriele, and daughter remained in the East, and after a quickie divorce organized by the state, Gabriele married a new boyfriend who, unbeknown to her, was a member of the Stasi. In 1983, after 53 appearances, Eigendorf was transferred from 1. FC Kaiserslautern to Eintracht Braunschweig. After just eight starts for his new club the moustachioed Eigendorf was fatally injured in a car accident on 5 March 1983. A postmortem showed a high level of alcohol in his bloodstream, but eyewitnesses who had seen him earlier that evening stated that he had drunk little. When the Stasi files were examined following German reunification they revealed that the footballer had been targeted for assassination by the sinister organization.

THE FIRST

MANAGER TO LEAD HIS TEAM UP THE STEPS TO THE WEMBLEY ROYAL BOX

BOB PAISLEY, LIVERPOOL V MANCHESTER UNITED AT WEMBLEY
STADIUM, MIDDLESEX, ENGLAND, 3 PM SATURDAY 26 MARCH 1983

Liverpool's most successful manager Bob Paisley made his 12th and last trip to Wembley for Liverpool's match against Manchester United in the League Cup in 1983. His players did him proud, winning the match and trophy by two goals to one, albeit needing extra time. To honour his achievements at Anfield the players let Paisley mount the 39 steps to the Royal Box before the captain Graeme Souness to collect the Cup after they beat United 2-1 after extra time to win their third consecutive League Cup. Liverpool were lucky to win – with a minute to play in the 90th goalkeeper Bruce Grobbelaar committed a professional foul on United's Gordon McQueen, but only received a yellow card. Referee George Courtney said that he didn't believe that McQueen had a scoring opportunity.

THE ONLY

FOOTBALLER TO MAKE HIS CUP DEBUT IN AN FA CUP FINAL

**Alan Davies, Manchester United v Brighton & Hove Albion at
Wembley Stadium, Middlesex, England, 3 pm Saturday 21 May 1983**

Alan Davies holds the unique position of being the only professional footballer to make his Cup debut in the Final. Ron Atkinson picked the little-known Welsh winger for the match, in which United were clear favourites, it being **Brighton & Hove Albion's FIRST appearance in an FA Cup Final**. The game ended in a two-all draw after extra time.

TO COIN A PHRASE

In the first match Brighton's Gordon Smith was through clear with only United keeper Gary Bailey to beat. Commentating for BBC Radio, Peter Jones declaimed, 'And Smith must score', only for Bailey to save. The words became the title of a Seagulls fanzine. Smith explained later that he didn't think that he would receive the ball from teammate Mike Robinson – 'I wasn't expecting a pass from Robbo. Robbo never passes.'

Brighton's goals came from Gordon Smith and Gary Stevens, while Frank Stapleton and Ray Wilkins furnished the goals for United. When the teams returned to Wembley, United showed their superior strength and won 4-0. Alan Davies was picked for the replay five days later, but only made seven appearances for United before his time was curtailed by injury and he was sold to Newcastle United for £65,000 in July 1985. In his career Davies won 11 caps for Wales, but made fewer than 200 League appearances in his career. On 4 February 1992 he committed suicide in his car near his South Wales home. He was 30 years old.

━•◆••◆•━

THE LAST
MEMBER OF ENGLAND 1966 WORLD CUP-WINNING TEAM
TO RETIRE FROM PLAYING
ALAN BALL, BRISTOL ROVERS V CARDIFF CITY AT BRISTOL STADIUM, EASTVILLE, BRISTOL, GLOUCESTERSHIRE, ENGLAND, SATURDAY 14 MAY 1983

Unsurprisingly, the youngest player was also the last one to quit playing. Midfielder Alan Ball was just 21 when he collected his winner's medal from the Queen. A month later he left Blackpool for Everton where he played 208 games and scored 66 goals. On 22 December 1971 he joined Arsenal where he became club captain. In 1973 Ball became the second England player sent off while playing in Warsaw against Poland. It was at Arsenal Stadium in 1975 that his England career came to an end with his 72nd cap, even though he was only 30. He had been appointed captain by manager Don Revie and then dropped without explanation after six matches.

MISSING THE MEDALS

The first three transfers of Alan Ball's career – to Everton (1966), Arsenal (1971) and Southampton (1976) – all came at a time when the clubs were FA Cup holders, but Ball never won a winner's medal.

In December 1976 Ball was sold to Southampton where he made 132 first team appearances, and then went to play for Philadelphia Fury in the USA in 1978 and on to Canada where he made 38 appearances for Vancouver Whitecaps. In February 1980 he became player-manager of his first club Blackpool, but it was not a success and he was sacked on 28 February 1981; the club was relegated at the end of the season. In March 1981 he returned to the south coast and Southampton where he played another 63 games before leaving in October 1982 to play for Hong Kong side Eastern Athletic. In January 1983 he began his last stint as a player with Bristol Rovers and played his last game – his 975th first team match – for them at the end of the season in a 1-1 draw. (See 1966, page 137).

THE FIRST

EUROPEAN CUP FINAL
TO GO TO PENALTIES

LIVERPOOL V AS ROMA AT STADIO OLIMPICO, ROME, ITALY, WEDNESDAY 30 MAY 1984

Liverpool's fourth victory in a European Cup Final was the first one that required penalties to decide the winner. After 120 minutes the score stood at 1-1, thanks to goals from Liverpool's Phil Neal in the 12th minute and an equalizer from Robert Pruzzo in the 42nd playing at Roma's own home ground, and Swedish referee Erik Fredriksson signalled the first penalty shoot-out in the European Cup Final. Steve Nicol, who had come on as a 72nd-minute substitute for Craig Johnston, missed the first penalty for Liverpool, but Roma's Agostino di Bartolomei netted for the Italians. Phil Neal slotted home his penalty before Bruno Conti missed. Graeme Souness, Ian Rush and Ray Kennedy all scored their penalties, while for Roma Ubaldo Righetti hit the back of the net and Francesco Graziani missed to send the trophy to Anfield in Joe Fagan's first season in charge.

THE LAST
HOME CHAMPIONSHIPS
1983–1984

The Home Championships came to an end when the Football Association declared that it wanted England to meet more talented or stronger teams. Scotland followed suit soon afterwards. Ironically, the weaker teams that England and Scotland didn't want to play triumphed in the final tournament. Northern Ireland won it and Wales finished second, England were third and the Scots last. The last match was between the auld enemies at Hampden Park, Glasgow on 26 May 1984 and the match ended in a 1-1 draw. Mark McGee scored the last goal for Scotland in the competition, while Tony Woodcock hit the last England strike. In all, England were champions 54 times (20 shared), Scotland 41 (17), Wales 12 (five) and Ireland/Northern Ireland eight (six). (See 1884, page 33 and 1980–1981, page 171).

THE ONLY
CLUB TO WIN A
MAJOR DOMESTIC TROPHY
AND BE RELEGATED IN SAME SEASON
NORWICH CITY, 1984–1985

Norwich faced mixed fortunes in 1984–1985. On 24 March 1985 they won the League Cup, beating Sunderland 1-0 at Wembley, although without scoring a final goal. It was an own goal by Gordon Chisholm (deflecting a shot by Asa Hartford) that sent the trophy to Carrow Road.

Later that season Norwich were relegated, finishing in 20th place in Division One with 49 points. Oddly, both finalists would have qualified for this entry, as Sunderland were also relegated, finishing one place and nine points behind Norwich. Gordon Chisholm as well as scoring an own goal set a record in that final – he became **the ONLY player to have played in the Scottish League Cup Final and the League Cup Final in the same year**. After the Final he was transferred to Hibernian where on 27 October he played in the Scottish League Cup Final against Aberdeen. Alex Ferguson's Dons won 3-0 (his ninth major trophy with the club). Chisholm thus became **the only player to have played in the Scottish League Cup Final and the League Cup Final in the same year and be on the losing side both times**.

THE FIRST

FA CUP FINAL
TO REALIZE £1 MILLION PLUS
AT THE GATE

Everton v Manchester United at Wembley Stadium, Middlesex, England, Saturday 18 May 1985

When the blues of Everton met the reds of Manchester United at Wembley it produced the first seven-figure receipts at the gate in an FA Cup Final – returning £1,100,000. Everton were the holders of the trophy and thus favourites, but it was United who went home with it, after Norman Whiteside scored in extra time. Had Everton won the match they would have completed an unprecedented treble of League title, FA and European Cup Winners' Cups. With 78 minutes gone Peter Reid headed for goal, only to be brought down by a professional foul from Kevin Moran of Manchester United, who became **the FIRST player to be shown a red card in an FA Cup Final** (by referee Peter Willis, whose full-time job was as a policeman) and had to be held back by teammate Frank Stapleton. All of United's players were full internationals, the first such FA Cup-winning team.

OTHER FIRSTS AND AN ONLY IN THIS MATCH:

The FIRST match in British football to return £1 million or more at the gate • The FIRST FA Cup-winning team with 11 internationals – all Manchester United's players were full internationals • The ONLY player sent off in an FA Cup Final

⎯◦•◦⎯

THE FIRST

LEAGUE CHAMPIONSHIP WON BY A
PLAYER-MANAGER

KENNY DALGLISH, LIVERPOOL, 1985–1986

On 10 August 1977 Bob Paisley paid Celtic a then record-breaking £440,000 to bring forward Kenny Dalglish to Liverpool after 204 League appearances at Parkhead. Paisley saw Dalglish as an ideal replacement for Kevin Keegan who had been sold to Hamburg. On 30 May 1985, after the retirement of Joe Fagan, Dalglish became the first player-manager of the club, breaking the tradition of appointing a back room boy to run Liverpool. The gamble proved a success, as Dalglish won not only the League but also the FA Cup, bringing the Double to Anfield for the first time and in his first season in charge. In his six years at the helm Liverpool always finished first or second. In his first season as player-manager Dalglish selected himself just 21 times, preferring to give younger players a chance, although he did pick himself for the FA Cup Final against Everton. Liverpool won 3-1 in **the FIRST all-Merseyside Final** and it was also **the first FA Cup Final-winning team with no Englishmen in the starting line-up**. There were four Scots, three Irishmen, a Dane, a Welshman, a Zimbabwean and an Australian. The only Englishman was substitute Steve McMahon. Dalglish announced his resignation to the board as manager on 21 February 1991 and went public the next day. On 3 July 2009 he rejoined the club as head of Liverpool's academy for young players. (See 1990, page 185).

THE SEASON ALSO SAW:

The FIRST Double won by a player-manager

THE FIRST

PLAYER TO RECEIVE THREE RED CARDS IN THE SAME MATCH

ALEX MILLER, ST MIRREN V MOTHERWELL AT ST MIRREN PARK, LOVE STREET, PAISLEY, RENFREWSHIRE, SCOTLAND, WEDNESDAY 29 OCTOBER 1986

Alex Miller holds an unenviable record. Playing for St Mirren he was sent off for fighting with one of the Motherwell players. He then received a second red card for arguing with the referee and a third red was shown for further dissent. One might think that Miller's record was unique, but it was repeated in December 2006 by another Scottish player, Andy McLaren, who was red carded three times playing for Dundee against Clyde.

THE FIRST

TEAM AUTOMATICALLY RELEGATED TO THE CONFERENCE LEAGUE

LINCOLN CITY, 1986–1987

At the end of the 1986–1987 season Lincoln City finished bottom of Division Four and in a new move became the first Football League club automatically relegated to the Conference League. It was the fourth time that they had been expelled from the Football League. They were voted out in 1908, again in 1911 and for a third time in 1920. In 1921 they became founder members of Division Three (North). They spent just one season in the Conference League before returning to the Football League. (See 1892, page 42).

THE FIRST
GOALKEEPER TO CAPTAIN
THE FA CUP WINNERS
Dave Beasant, Wimbledon v Liverpool at Wembley Stadium, Middlesex,
England, 3 pm Saturday 14 May 1988

Wimbledon's curly-headed keeper led the team out for their only FA Cup Final in 1988. Lawrie Sanchez scored the only goal of the game eight minutes from half-time. With 60 minutes gone Clive Goodyear of the Crazy Gang conceded a penalty, bringing down John Aldridge. Determined not to spoil his own day, Beasant dived to his left to save Aldridge's effort. Fifteen years later, in his last match for Arsenal, David Seaman donned the captain's armband as the Gunners defeated Southampton in **the First indoors Cup Final**. Coincidentally, both matches ended 1-0.

ANOTHER FIRST AND AN ONLY IN THIS MATCH:
The FIRST goalkeeper to save a penalty in an FA Cup Final
• The ONLY FA Cup Final win for Wimbledon

THE FIRST
CHAIRMAN-MANAGER
OF A BRITISH CLUB
Jim McLean, Dundee United, Tannadice Park, Tannadice Street,
Dundee, Scotland, Tuesday 20 December 1988

Having spent three years playing for rivals Dundee, it came as something of a surprise for Dundee United fans when Jim McLean became their manager in December 1971. In 1974 he led the Terrors to their first Scottish Cup Final, although they lost 3-0 to Celtic. In December 1979 United won the League Cup and retained it the following season. Dundee United won the Scottish Premier Division title for the first time in the club's history in 1982–1983 with what was at the time a record number of points and goals scored. Rangers then offered McLean a job, but he turned them down, as he did with an offer in June 1984 from Newcastle

United. That year he became a director at Tannadice Park and in 1988 became chairman and managing director, while still remaining manager. He kept the managerial position until July 1993 and stayed as chairman until October 2000. He sold his 42 per cent stake in the club to Eddie Thompson in October 2002, but was later bitterly critical of Thompson's stewardship of Dundee United.

THE FIRST
MANAGER OF TWO EUROPEAN CUP WINNERS' CUP-WINNING TEAMS
JOHAN CRUYFF, AJAX V LOKOMOTIV LEIPZIG AT SPIROS LOUIS (OLYMPIC) STADIUM, ATHENS, GREECE, WEDNESDAY 13 MAY 1987; BARCELONA V SAMPDORIA AT WANKDORF STADIUM, BERN, SWITZERLAND, WEDNESDAY 10 MAY 1989

Following his huge success as a player, Johan Cruyff became a triumph as a manager. He was the first man to lead two separate teams to victory in the European Cup Winners' Cup. The first was an all-Dutch Ajax side, and a Marco van Basten goal in the 21st minute gave them the title against the East Germans from Lokomotiv Leipzig. The second side that Cruyff led to the ECWC Final was Barcelona, who beat Sampdoria from Italy 2-0 in the Final. Barcelona fielded nine Spaniards in their line-up; the only two foreigners were right back Aloísio from Brazil and a forward by the name of Gary Lineker. The five players on the bench were all Spanish as well. Oddly, Cruyff had played for both the clubs he later managed.

THE ONLY
TIME THE LEAGUE TITLE WAS DECIDED BY THE LAST KICK OF THE SEASON
ARSENAL V LIVERPOOL AT ANFIELD, SEAFORTH, LIVERPOOL, MERSEYSIDE, ENGLAND, FRIDAY 26 MAY 1989

Often the Football League title is decided long before the end of the season. Sometimes it goes to the last day of the season and it hangs on the relative results of different matches. But on 26 May 1989 it was decided, Cup Final-like, by the result of one game – the last match of the season, between title contenders Liverpool and Arsenal. Except that, unlike a Cup Final, Arsenal had to win by at least two goals to claim the title at Anfield against a team that had recently beaten local rivals Everton in the FA Cup Final to set up the possibility of an unprecedented second Double. As expected it was a hard-fought contest. At half-time the scores were still deadlocked at 0-0. Then seven minutes into the second half Arsenal scored from a disputed free kick. The League title now rested on a single goal – or the lack of one. Liverpool were not just defending their goal mouth, they were defending their League title and their double Double. There was no way through for Arsenal. Or so it seemed... With seconds of the match to play, Lee Dixon collected the ball and passed up field to Alan Smith. Alan Smith passed to Michael Thomas. Thomas outwitted Steve Nicol. Only Grobbelaar to beat. Grobbelaar came out to challenge Thomas, and Thomas flicked it over the Zimbabwean keeper for what has been called the most dramatic goal in Football League history: 2-0 and the League Championship to Arsenal.

THE LAST

MATCH AS A PLAYER FOR
KENNY DALGLISH

LIVERPOOL V DERBY COUNTY AT ANFIELD, SEAFORTH, LIVERPOOL,
MERSEYSIDE, ENGLAND, TUESDAY 1 MAY 1990

Having become player-manager in May 1985, Dalglish played just 21 times in 1985–1986 and cut back further on his appearances as he gave preference to younger players. He didn't play at all in 1988–1989, but on the last home game of the next season wearing the number 14 shirt he brought himself on as a 71st-minute substitute (replacing number seven Jan Molby) in a match against Derby County before announcing his retirement from playing. At the end of the match Liverpool were crowned Division One champions, having won 1-0. (See 1985, page 181).

THE FIRST
PLAYER SENT OFF
IN A WORLD CUP FINAL

PEDRO MONZÓN, ARGENTINA V WEST GERMANY AT STADIO, OLIMPICO ROME, ITALY, 8 PM SUNDAY 8 JULY 1990

Around 74,000 spectators crowded into Rome's Olympic Stadium to watch the 13th World Cup Final between one team managed by World Cup winner Franz Beckenbauer and the other captained by cheating junkie Diego Maradona who received a yellow card three minutes before full-time. A tightly fought match was enlivened by the sending off of Pedro Monzón in the 65th minute (he had only come on as a half-time substitute), followed by his teammate Gustavo Dezotti 22 minutes later. The only goal of the game came from the penalty spot courtesy of Andreas Brehme two minutes before Dezotti's dismissal.

IN THIS MATCH ARGENTINA BECAME: The FIRST team to have two players sent off in a World Cup Final

THE LAST
INTERNATIONAL
PLAYED BY EAST GERMANY

BELGIUM V EAST GERMANY AT CONSTANT VANDEN STOCK STADIUM, BRUSSELS, BELGIUM, WEDNESDAY 12 SEPTEMBER 1990

With the unification of Germany on 3 October 1990 the two nation's teams merged into one. Eight months earlier, on 2 February 1990, the draw for Euro '92 had been made and East Germany had been drawn in Group 5 alongside Belgium, Wales, Luxembourg and West Germany. The arrangements for the first qualifying match against Belgium were too far advanced to be cancelled, so East Germany's last international was altered to be a friendly in Brussels. The East Germans won 2-0 with two goals in the second half from Matthias Sammer. The last East German team comprised Jens Schmidt (substituted for Jens Adler in the 90th minute), Heiko Peschke, Jörg Schwanke, Andreas Wagenhaus, Detlef Schössler, Matthias Sammer, Jörg Stübner (replaced by Stefan Böger in the 25th minute), Dariusz Wosz, Heiko Bonan, Heiko Scholz (substituted in the 85th minute by Torsten Kracht) and Uwe Rösler. The intended qualifying match between East Germany and West Germany, slated for Leipzig on 14 November 1990, was then rescheduled as a friendly to celebrate the unification. However, rioting in East Germany forced the match to be abandoned before a ball had been kicked.

THE FIRST

PLAYER SENT OFF
FROM THE BENCH

BEN ROWE, EXETER CITY V FULHAM AT CRAVEN COTTAGE, STEVENAGE ROAD, LONDON, ENGLAND, SATURDAY 27 OCTOBER 1990

Players expect comments from fans and there is not a lot they or the referee can do about it. This was not the case with Exeter's Ben Rowe, who was vociferous in his criticism – so much so that even though he was sitting on the subs' bench the referee showed him a red card for dissent.

THE LAST

DIVISION ONE CHAMPIONS

Leeds United, 1991–1992

The last winners of the old Division One were the Howard Wilkinson-managed Leeds United who attained 82 points from their 42 games, beating Manchester United (78 points) into second place. The triumph, the first for the club in 18 years, came on 26 April 1992 just two seasons after Leeds had been promoted to Division One. The trophy that was presented to Leeds became the one given to the winners of Division One, now the Championship. (See 1999, 2000, page 209).

WITH THIS VICTORY, HOWARD WILKINSON BECAME: The LAST Englishman to manage a team that won the League Championship

THE FIRST

TIME THE FA CUP LOSERS COLLECTED THEIR MEDALS FIRST

LIVERPOOL V SUNDERLAND AT WEMBLEY STADIUM, MIDDLESEX, ENGLAND, 3 PM SATURDAY 9 MAY 1992

It had been a Wembley tradition for many years for the winners to ascend the 39 steps to the Royal Box first to collect the Cup and their medals. For the first time in 1992 Sunderland, the losing side by two goals to nil, went up first to collect their losers' medals from the Duke of Kent. Then they were given the winners' medals by mistake and had the embarrassment of having to swap on the pitch before the laps of honour, and in the dressing rooms afterwards.

When the first FA Cup was stolen, a second one was commissioned and on 6 February 1911 was presented to 3rd Baron Kinnaird in recognition of his 33 years as president of the FA, a third one being prepared in time for the 1911 FA Cup Final. By the beginning of the 1990s the trophy had become very fragile and the Football Association arranged for an exact copy to be made. It was this that was first presented at the 1992 Final, while the original was kept safely in a bank vault. On 10 May 1992 Phil Thompson, Liverpool's reserve team coach, dropped the lid as he left the team hotel. It was dented and did not fit properly.

ANOTHER FIRST AND AN ONLY IN THIS MATCH:
The FIRST presentation of the 'new' FA Cup • The ONLY time FA Cup losers were given winners' medals by mistake

THE FIRST

TIME ENGLAND WORE THEIR NAMES ON THE
BACK OF THEIR SHIRTS

European Championship, Sweden, 1992

The first time that England's players wore their names on the back of their shirts was on 11 June 1992 at Malmö, Sweden in Euro '92. They retained the numbers 1–11, but had their surnames on the back of their shirts. It was not a happy experience for the team. They drew their opening match 0-0 with Denmark and then played out another goalless draw with France three days later before losing their last match to hosts Sweden 2-1 on 17 June and catching the plane home.

THE LAST

INTERNATIONAL MATCH FOR
GARY LINEKER

ENGLAND V SWEDEN AT RÅSUNDASTADION, STOCKHOLM,
SWEDEN, WEDNESDAY 17 JUNE 1992

Future television presenter Gary Lineker's last international game was in the last match of England's Euro '92 campaign. Playing against hosts Sweden, David Platt of Juventus scored after just three minutes and that was the way the score stayed at half-time. Then Jan Eriksson equalized for Sweden on 51 minutes. In the 64th minute manager Graham Taylor pulled off his captain and centre forward Lineker, winning his 80th cap, and replaced him with Alan Smith of Arsenal who was winning his 13th and last cap. Another Arsenal man, Paul Merson, came on in the 79th minute to replace Andy Sinton of Queens Park Rangers, but three minutes later Thomas Brolin scored Sweden's second and winning goal. After the match Lineker announced his immediate retirement from international football. The man who was never booked had scored 48 goals for his country, which left him one short of Bobby Charlton's record of 49 goals.

THE LAST
MATCH PLAYED BY
ROY OF THE ROVERS

MELCHESTER ROVERS V REDSTOKE AT MEL PARK, MELCHESTER,
ENGLAND, MARCH 1993

While playing for Milston Youth Club's football side on 11 September 1954, 15-year-old Roy Race was spotted by Melchester Rovers scout Alf Leeds. In August 1955 Race and his best friend Blackie Gray made their first team debuts against Elbury Wanderers. Through triumph and adversity (mostly the former) over the next decades, Race and Melchester Rovers battled through to win almost every honour the game has to offer. Race eventually became player-manager, manager and then owner of the club, scoring ten goals in eight FA Cup Final wins between 1959 and 1990. From 25 September 1976 until 20 March 1993 he even had his own weekly comic devoted to his adventures, and then from September 1993 until March 1995 a monthly.

In October 1992 Race announced that he was standing down as manager but would continue to play. The board appointed Ralph Gordon who had spent ten trophyless years at rivals Melboro. In March 1993 Melchester played Redstoke and won 4-0, and Race was reinstated as manager. After the game Melchester chief scout Charlie Madden told Race about a potential new signing, Darren Lewis. Tragically, Race's helicopter crashed and he hovered near death for several months at Melchester General Hospital. He survived, however, although his left foot – 'Race's Rocket' – had to be amputated. His playing career was finally over at 53 – eat your heart out Stanley Matthews.

—•••—

THE FIRST
PREMIER LEAGUE CHAMPIONS

MANCHESTER UNITED, SUNDAY 2 MAY 1993

When the 1990–1991 season came to an end the leading clubs in the country established what would become the Premier League with the

Founder Members Agreement, which was signed on 17 July 1991. It was argued that the increased revenue from television and other sources would allow English teams to compete at the highest level in Europe. In 1992 all the clubs in Division One resigned en masse from the Football League, and on 27 May the FA Premier League was formed, signalling the end of the 104-year-old Football League, as it had been known. The 22 inaugural members of the Premier League in 1992–1993 were Arsenal, Aston Villa, Blackburn Rovers, Chelsea, Coventry City, Crystal Palace, Everton, Ipswich Town, Leeds United, Liverpool, Manchester City, Manchester United, Middlesbrough, Norwich City, Nottingham Forest, Oldham Athletic, Queens Park Rangers, Sheffield United, Sheffield Wednesday, Southampton, Tottenham Hotspur and Wimbledon. The first champions were Manchester United and they have dominated the Premier League since. Ferguson was relaxing on the golf course when he learned that his nearest rivals Aston Villa had lost at Oldham Athletic to send the trophy to Old Trafford. Ironically, Brian Deane of Sheffield United scored **the FIRST Premier League goal** in a 2-1 win against Manchester United.

In the 17 years since its formation only four clubs have won the Premier League – Arsenal, Blackburn Rovers, Chelsea and Manchester United – and none have been managed by an Englishman. The Premier League, which has been sponsored since 1993, was reduced to 20 clubs in 1995 when four teams were relegated and only two promoted.

THE FIRST
SIDE TO WIN BOTH
THE FA CUP AND THE LEAGUE CUP
IN THE SAME SEASON
ARSENAL V SHEFFIELD WEDNESDAY AT WEMBLEY STADIUM, MIDDLESEX, ENGLAND, 1992–1993

In 1992–1993 Arsenal created history by becoming the first team to win both major domestic cup competitions in the same season. In addition, oddly, their opponents on both occasions were Sheffield Wednesday and on both occasions the result was 2-1 to the Gunners. The first match, the League Cup Final, was staged at Wembley before 74,007 fans on 18 April

1993. Arsenal's goals came from Paul Merson and Steve Morrow (his first for the club at senior level), although 22-year-old Morrow was unable to enjoy most of the post-match celebrations. At the final whistle the captain Tony Adams had picked Morrow up and promptly dropped him, breaking his arm in the process and necessitating oxygen for the utility player. This game was **the FIRST match in which any European clubs had used squad numbers on their shirts instead of the usual 1–11**.

On 15 May 1993 the Gunners and the Owls met again at Wembley for the second Cup Final of the season. This time 79,347 fans watched the two teams play out a one-all draw (after extra time) in the FA Cup Final, with Arsenal's solitary goal coming from Ian Wright who was playing with a broken toe. Luckily, he scored with his head. This was the **FIRST FA Cup Final in which squad numbers had been used**, having been trialled in the League Cup Final. Players from both clubs used the same numbers for all three matches. The Premier League adopted the system for the following season. On 20 May Arsenal and Sheffield Wednesday returned to Wembley for the FA Cup Final replay.

Both FA Cup Semi-Finals were staged at Wembley, so the Gunners and the Owls each played there four times in six weeks – FA Cup Semi-Final, League Cup Final, FA Cup Final and replay. The replay attracted the smallest crowd (62,267) for an FA Cup Final at Wembley. The kick-off was put back half an hour because a crash on the M1 had delayed thousands of Wednesday fans. It was the first time a Wembley match had not kicked off on time since the White Horse Final in 1923. It was also raining heavily. In the early stages Mark Bright went in roughly on Andy Linighan and broke the Arsenal man's nose. Ian Wright opened the scoring on 34 minutes putting Arsenal ahead, as he had done in the first

---

FAN FURY

Owls fan Bob Montgomery was so annoyed by what he believed was an under par performance from Sheffield Wednesday in the FA Cup Final that he sued the club under the Trades Description Act. He claimed that they had obtained money under false pretences. Sadly for him, but probably luckily for other football clubs besides Wednesday, he lost his case.

game, but after 61 minutes Chris Waddle equalized for Wednesday and that was the way it stayed at 90 minutes. With just a minute of extra time remaining Andy Linighan won the game for Arsenal with a header. Liverpool repeated this feat of winning League and FA Cups in 2001, as did Chelsea in 2007.

THE ONLY
FOOTBALL LEAGUE TEAM
TO HAVE TWO GOALKEEPERS SENT OFF
COLCHESTER UNITED V HEREFORD UNITED AT LAYER ROAD GROUND, COLCHESTER, ESSEX, ENGLAND, SATURDAY 16 OCTOBER 1993

In the Division Three match between Colchester United and Hereford United, Us' goalie John Keeley was sent off for committing a professional foul. Manager Roy McDonough replaced Steve Brown with the reserve goalie Nathan Munson. He fared no better than the first choice and was also sent off for committing a professional foul. Unsurprisingly, Colchester lost the game 5-0.

THE ONLY
INTERNATIONAL CANCELLED
BECAUSE IT COINCIDED WITH HITLER'S BIRTHDAY
Germany v England at Hamburg/Olympic Stadium, Berlin, Germany, Wednesday 20 April 1994

The German Football Association scheduled a friendly against England in the spring of 1994 without apparently realizing that the date chosen happened to be the 105th anniversary of Adolf Hitler's birthday. The English Football Association refused to play, saying that there was too much danger of violence. FA president Sir Bert Millichip commented:

'For a period of over three months, since this match was moved to Berlin, we have been fully aware of the risks of disorder. We had hoped that these risks might

have receded. Unfortunately, in our opinion, they have not. I am sure that as soon as there is an acceptable date, another friendly match will be arranged.'

The match was originally to have been held in Hamburg, but local police said that they could not provide enough security. Berlin officials volunteered to play host for the game, and scheduled it for the Olympic Stadium, which was built by Hitler's government for the 1936 Olympics. The German authorities were angered by the English decision. Otto Johne, the head of the Berlin branch of Germany's football federation, put it like this:

'It's an outrage. We are extremely disappointed and depressed by this decision. It's bad for sport when a tiny minority of extremists succeed like this. They're making 20 April a day of glory for the Nazis again.'

German goalkeeping legend Sepp Maier deplored the action and said that English officials were 'playing right into the hands of the hooligans', while Gordon Banks said the decision 'makes me angry because we are bowing down to a minority, a very small minority'. However, Gordon Taylor, the chief executive of the Professional Footballers' Association, concluded, 'To consider it in the first place was a gross error of judgment.'

THE FIRST
WORLD CUP FINALS
TO HAVE NAMES PRINTED ON THE BACK OF
PLAYERS' SHIRTS
United States of America, 1994

These Finals were the first time that players had their names printed on the back of their jerseys in a World Cup, just like other American sports did. This custom followed from Euro '92, and has continued ever since. The USA has tried several times to get its people interested in soccer and this World Cup did nothing to change that. They still prefer baseball and American football, but the matches did have the highest average World Cup attendances to date. No team from the UK qualified for the tournament, the first such occurrence since they began entering.

THE FIRST

WORLD CUP MATCH
PLAYED INDOORS

**UNITED STATES OF AMERICA V SWITZERLAND, PONTIAC
SILVERDOME, 1200 FEATHERSTONE ROAD, PONTIAC, MICHIGAN,
UNITED STATES OF AMERICA, SATURDAY 18 JUNE 1994**

The United States–Switzerland match in the Pontiac Silverdome was the first played indoors in World Cup history: the grass was grown by Michigan State University and was the first time since 1965 that natural turf was used in an indoor stadium in the USA. It was Switzerland's first Finals match since 1966. The match ended with the teams sharing two goals, both scored from free kicks. Georges Brégy scored for the Swiss on 39 minutes and Eric Wynalda equalized for the Americans on the stroke of half-time.

THE FIRST

PLAYER TO SCORE
FIVE GOALS IN A
SINGLE WORLD CUP FINALS GAME

OLEG SALENKO, RUSSIA V CAMEROON AT STANFORD STADIUM, ARBORETUM ROAD & GALVEZ STREET, STANFORD, CALIFORNIA, UNITED STATES OF AMERICA, 4 PM TUESDAY 28 JUNE 1994

Oleg Salenko of Russia became the team hero in his country's group stage 6-1 win over Cameroon before 74,914 spectators. Salenko, 24, hit the back of the net in the 15th, 41st, 44th (a penalty), 72nd and 75th minutes. Dmitri Radchenko scored nine minutes from time, while Cameroon's solitary effort came from Roger Milla who, at 42 years and 39 days, became the oldest player in the World Cup and consequently the oldest scorer.

THE ONLY

PLAYER MURDERED
AFTER SCORING AN OWN GOAL
IN A WORLD CUP MATCH

ANDRÉS ESCOBAR, MEDELLÍN, COLOMBIA, SATURDAY 2 JULY 1994

Prior to the World Cup Colombia had been a favoured team and it was reported that heavy bets – many by the powerful drug syndicates that run Colombia – had been placed on the team doing well. Footballing legend Pelé even tipped them to win the trophy. However, the plaudits placed undue pressure on the team and manager Hernan Gomez was reported to have received death threats over matters of team selection. On 22 June 1994 Colombia played the United States of America at the Pasadena Rose Bowl before 93,689 spectators. It was the fourth match in Group A and the second game for both countries. The USA had drawn their opening match, while Romania had comprehensively beaten Colombia 3-1 in their first game, so it was important for both sides to win. On the 34th minute America attacked and midfielder John Harkes crossed the ball. Attempting to block the cross, sweeper Andrés Escobar slid forward and rather than clearing the ball managed to put it into his own net. Seven minutes after half-time Earnie Stewart made it 2-0 to America. Colombia managed a consolation goal through Adolfo Valencia with a minute on the clock, but it was not enough and despite a win in their final match against Switzerland it meant an early plane home for the team, who finished bottom of the group.

Ten days after his own goal Escobar visited the El Indio bar in a suburb of Medellín. As he left he was approached by a man who shot him 12 times, reportedly yelling 'Goal!' after delivering each bullet. Escobar, a popular figure in Colombia, was given a hero's funeral, which was attended by 120,000 people. On 30 June 1995 Humberto Castro Muñoz, a local schoolmaster, was found guilty of Escobar's murder and sentenced to 43 years' imprisonment. The punishment was later reduced to 26 years and Castro was released in October 2005.

THE FIRST

WORLD CUP FINAL
DECIDED ON PENALTIES

**BRAZIL V ITALY AT ROSE BOWL, 1001 ROSE BOWL DRIVE, PASADENA, CALIFORNIA,
UNITED STATES OF AMERICA, 12.35 PM SUNDAY 17 JULY 1994**

No strangers to facing each other in the World Cup Final, Brazil and Italy played out a goalless draw after extra time before 94,194 spectators at California's Rose Bowl in 1994. When referee Sándor Puhl of Hungary blew his whistle after extra time, history was made as the two teams lined up to take penalties. Franco Baresi stepped up to take the first penalty for Italy and promptly hit it over the bar. Brazil's first taker, Márcio Santos, saw Italian keeper Gianluca Pagliuca save it. Demetrio Albertini scored to make it 1-0 to Italy. Romário scored for Brazil – 1-1. Alberigo Evani also hit the back of the net – 2-1 Italy. Next up was Branco – 2-2. Daniele Massaro then saw his effort saved by Brazilian goalie Claudio Taffarel. Dunga converted his penalty to give the Brazilians a 3-2 lead, with the final responsibility weighing on the shoulders of Roberto Baggio. The pressure was too much for the Divine Ponytail and he skyed the ball over the bar. The World Cup was Brazil's for a fourth time.

THE ONLY

BRITISH PLAYER
WHOSE NAME WAS ADOPTED BY AN
ITALIAN ANARCHIST COLLECTIVE

LUTHER BLISSETT, ITALY, MONDAY 7 NOVEMBER 1994

Watford forward Luther Blissett signed for AC Milan in June 1983 for a fee of £1.2 million, but his time in Italy was not a success – he scored just five goals in 30 appearances and was sold back to Watford after a year.

Rumours persist that Milan had mistakenly signed Blissett when really they wanted John Barnes. On 7 November 1994 the Luther Blissett Project was first mentioned on Usenet (an online bulletin board) and the name has since been used by a collective of anarchists including artists, performers, poets, squatters and underground reviews. On 30 June 2004 Blissett appeared on television and proclaimed, *'Chiunque può essere Luther Blissett, semplicemente adottando il nome Luther Blissett.'* ('Anyone can be Luther Blissett simply by adopting the name Luther Blissett.') Four artists associated with the Luther Blissett Project wrote the novel *Q* under the pseudonym Luther Blissett, which became an international bestseller.

THE ONLY
FOOTBALL LEAGUE PLAYER
JAILED FOR
ATTACKING A SUPPORTER

Eric Cantona, Manchester United v Crystal Palace at Selhurst Park, London, England, Wednesday 25 January 1995

During his time in English football Eric Cantona amazed many, puzzled not a few and astounded a good number. Playing for Manchester United in a 1-1 draw against Crystal Palace he was sent off for a foul. As he was leaving the pitch he became fed up with the taunts of Palace supporters, one in particular, and flung himself at the mouthy fan feet first. For his behaviour Cantona was charged with bringing the game into disrepute, fined £20,000 and banned for eight months from playing. Cantona was also jailed for two weeks, although on appeal that sentence was reduced to 120 hours' community service. Former player Jimmy Greaves quipped, 'Eric Cantona was sentenced to 120 hours' community service, which has been reduced to 80 hours on appeal – from the community.' (See 1996, page 201).

THE LAST

MATCH AT AYRESOME PARK

**Middlesbrough v Luton Town at Ayresome Park, Middlesbrough,
Cleveland, England, Saturday 30 April 1995**

Formed at the Albert Park Hotel in 1876 by members of the
Middlesbrough Cricket Club, Middlesbrough Association, as they then
were, began playing at the Archery Ground in Albert Park. Their first
match was against a rugby team, Tees Wanderers, and the match ended
with a goal apiece. Jackson Ewbank scored Middlesbrough's first goal.
They moved to a field on Breckon Hill Road and stayed there for a
season before moving on to Linthorpe Road West cricket ground in 1879
where they remained until 1903. A breakaway club was formed,
Middlesbrough Ironopolis, and both turned professional in 1889.
Middlesbrough reverted to amateur status in 1892, a year before
Middlesbrough Ironopolis were elected to Division Two of the Football
League. They folded after just a season. When Boro were elected to the
Football League in 1899, they realized that they would need somewhere
more suited to a top-flight club. Their first League match at Linthorpe
Road was a Division Two game against Small Heath (later Birmingham
City), who won 3-1. Ayresome Park was built at Oldgate Farm and
Paradise Field. To build the stadium a community of gypsies had to be
moved and legend has it that they placed a curse on the club that they
would never win a trophy while in residence.

The new 274 ft (83.5 m) long stand was designed by Glasgow architect
Archibald Leitch, who had worked and would work on several top stadia.
The other stand was brought from the Linthorpe Road West cricket
ground to the south side of Ayresome Park. The stadium cost £11,957, a
sum that was largely financed by loans. **The FIRST match played at
Ayresome Park** was a friendly game against Celtic on 1 September. **The
FIRST competitive match** was played on 12 September 1903 against
Sunderland in Division One. Middlesbrough's Joe Cassidy scored **the
FIRST goal at Ayresome Park**, but the Wearsiders won 3-2. Standing
cost 6d and if you wanted a seat that was 9d extra. In 1966 Ayresome Park

was one of the chosen venues to host World Cup matches and it saw three involving the Soviet Union, North Korea, Italy and Chile.

As with other stadia, the Taylor Report did for Ayresome Park and the last competitive match played there was the final home match of the 1994–1995 season before 23,903 spectators. Middlesbrough won 2-1, with both goals coming from John Hendrie – it was the season that Boro won the Division One title to get promotion to the Premier League. Ayresome Park was demolished in early 1997. The site of the stadium is now a housing estate. The very last match at the ground was a testimonial match for Stephen Pears, who scored **the LAST goal at the venue** (from the penalty spot). From the start of the 1995–1996 season Middlesbrough played at the Riverside Stadium.

THE ONLY
CLUB CHAIRMAN TO ATTEMPT TO
BURN DOWN HIS OWN GROUND
KEN RICHARDSON, DONCASTER ROVERS, BELLE VUE GROUND, DONCASTER, SOUTH YORKSHIRE, ENGLAND, THURSDAY 29 JUNE 1995

At the end of June in 1995 the main stand at Belle Vue caught fire, causing damage estimated at £100,000. It emerged that Doncaster owner-chairman (or, as he insisted on being known, 'benefactor') Ken Richardson had paid former SAS soldier Alan Kristiansen £10,000 to start the blaze. The plot came to light after Kristiansen, not showing the usual professionalism expected of the SAS, was traced after he left his mobile at the scene and arrested. Police took Richardson into custody when the full-time whistle blew at a match against Fulham on 25 March 1996 and he went on trial at Sheffield Crown Court on 7 January 1999. According to the prosecution Richardson had wanted Doncaster to leave Belle Vue for a new ground. Gilbert Gray QC, Richardson's barrister, told the court that his client wanted only the best for the club. 'Was this a greedy man seeking to make a huge killing out of insurance? The answer is no,' he said. 'What it could have achieved was a move for the club.'

On 27 January Richardson was found guilty and, on 5 March,

sentenced to four years' imprisonment. On the same day Kristiansen, 41, was jailed for 12 months for conspiracy to commit arson. Two other men who helped him to start the fire – Ian Hay, 54, from Gateshead, and Alan Cracknall, 32, of Ryton, Newcastle – pleaded guilty to arson. Both were sentenced to nine months, suspended for two years. It was not the first time that Richardson had been in trouble. In 1984 he was given a nine-month suspended sentence and fined £20,000 for his part in a racing scandal known as the Flockton Grey affair. (See 2006, page 218).

THE FIRST
FRENCHMAN
TO CAPTAIN THE FA CUP WINNERS

ERIC CANTONA, MANCHESTER UNITED V LIVERPOOL AT WEMBLEY STADIUM, MIDDLESEX, ENGLAND, SATURDAY 11 MAY 1996

The sometimes volatile, occasionally eccentric Eric Cantona was the first of his countrymen to captain an FA Cup-winning team. The Frenchman, who was also Footballer of the Year, led Manchester United in their ninth successful campaign when they were **the FIRST team to do the Double twice.** At Wembley Cantona scored the only goal of the game five minutes from time in a match where Liverpool never really looked like hitting the back of the United net. (See 1995, page 198).

THE ONLY
INTERNATIONAL MATCH
WITHOUT OPPOSITION

ESTONIA V SCOTLAND AT KADRIORU STADIUM, TALINN, ESTONIA, 3 PM WEDNESDAY 9 OCTOBER 1996

Estonia and Scotland were drawn in the same qualifying group (number four) for the 1998 World Cup and a match was scheduled for the Kadrioru Stadium at Talinn. The night before the game the Scotland squad trained at the ground, but were disappointed by the quality of the temporary floodlights, which were mounted on the back of lorries. They complained to the Fifa delegation and the time of the kick-off was brought forward from 6.45 pm to 3 pm. This annoyed the Estonians who didn't bother to go to the ground. Scotland turned up, got changed and took to the pitch to cheers from their own supporters who sang, accurately, 'There's only one team in Talinn, one team in Talinn'. There was no opposition. The Yugoslavian referee Miroslav Radoman didn't toss a coin, perhaps fearing that Scotland captain John Collins would call wrongly. He blew his whistle to start the match, Billy Dodds of Scotland kicked off and passed to Collins and Radoman immediately abandoned the game. At 5 pm Estonia arrived at the ground. The match was referred to Fifa who made a quick decision a month later on 7 November and ordered it replayed in Monaco. The two teams played out a goalless draw at 8 pm on 11 February 1997 at the Louis II Stadium.

THE LAST
MATCH AT BURNDEN PARK

BOLTON WANDERERS V CHARLTON ATHLETIC AT BURNDEN PARK, BOLTON, LANCASHIRE, ENGLAND, FRIDAY 25 APRIL 1997

The first Football League substitute came onto the field at Burnden Park in a match between Bolton and Charlton Athletic, so perhaps it was fitting that the two teams met again for the final match at the stadium that had been Bolton's home since 1895. Bolton were already Division One champions when the Addicks arrived and it seemed as if the visitors wanted to ruin the celebrations by going 1-0 up by half-time. The Trotters fought back in the second half and won the match 4-1, with the last goal being scored by John McGinlay. Bolton were presented with the trophy and the crowd sang *Auld Lang Syne* before leaving the ground for the last time. Burnden Park was knocked down in 1999 and Bolton moved to the Reebok Stadium. Before its redevelopment Burnden Park fell into disrepair and gypsies set up an illegal camp on the site. Now a large Asda occupies the area and has pictures of the old stadium above the checkouts.

THE LAST
MATCH AT ROKER PARK
SUNDERLAND V EVERTON AT ROKER PARK, SUNDERLAND, TYNE & WEAR, ENGLAND, 3 PM SATURDAY 3 MAY 1997

Sunderland moved from Newcastle Road to Roker Park in 1898 with the ground being officially opened by Charles Vane-Tempest-Stewart, 6th Marquess of Londonderry, on 10 September of that year. The stadium had been built in quick time with the wooden stand taking just three months to complete. The turf was imported from Ireland and lasted for 37 years. The pitch was 1 ft (30 cm) higher in the middle than the ends to help with drainage. The first match played was a friendly against Liverpool and the Black Cats won 1-0, with Jim Leslie scoring **the First goal at the new ground**. In the 1930s the capacity rose to 60,000, but one game saw 75,118 in attendance. During the Second World War a bomb landed on the pitch, killing a policeman who was walking past. In 1952 Roker Park became the second ground (after Arsenal Stadium) fitted with floodlights. When the Taylor Report recommended all-seater stadia, Sunderland realized that they couldn't (like Arsenal) expand sufficiently and began looking for a new ground. In 1997 Sunderland relocated to the Stadium of Light, in nearby Monkwearmouth, on the site of the closed Monkwearmouth Colliery. The last competitive match at the ground was a 3-0 victory over Everton before 22,108 spectators, although it was not enough to prevent Sunderland being relegated. After the match Charlie Hurley (voted the club's Player of the Century) dug up the centre spot of the ground for it to be replanted at the new stadium.

FOOTIELAND

Roker Park was demolished and a housing estate built on the land. To commemorate the old ground the streets were named Promotion Close, Clockstand Close, Goalmouth Close, Midfield Drive and Roker Park Close.

THE FIRST
FOREIGN MANAGER
TO WIN A DOMESTIC TROPHY IN ENGLAND
RUUD GULLIT, 1997

On 17 May 1997 Ruud Gullit became the first foreigner to manage a team that won a major domestic trophy when his Chelsea side won the FA Cup, beating Middlesbrough 2-0 in the final. Roberto di Matteo and Eddie Newton scored Chelsea's goals.

THE LAST
CLUB TO WEAR 'NORMAL' NUMBERS
IN THE PREMIER LEAGUE
Charlton Athletic v Southampton at The Valley, Floyd Road, Charlton, London, England, Saturday 22 August 1998

With the advent of the Premier League came the rampant commercialism of football. As well as selling rights to television broadcasters, clubs realized that they could also make money from fans buying replica shirts. For a few pounds more the fan could have the name and number of their favourite player on the back of the shirt, but what if the player wore number eight one week and nine the following? Thus were born squad numbers. The last team in the Premier League to wear shirts numbered from 1–11 were Charlton Athletic in their first two games of the 1998–1999 season before they too reverted to squad numbers. They won the last match 5-0.

THE FIRST
FOREIGN MANAGER TO WIN THE PREMIERSHIP
Arsène Wenger OBE, Arsenal, 1998

Born at Strasbourg on 22 October 1949, Arsenal's longest-serving and most successful manager Arsène Wenger joined the club from the Japanese side Nagoya Grampas 8 on 1 October 1996. His first match in charge was a 2-0 victory over Blackburn Rovers on 12 October 1996, and he won the Double for the club in his first full season as manager. The Premiership title came with a convincing 4-0 win over Everton at Highbury. A fortnight later they beat Newcastle United 2-0 in the FA Cup Final, which was **the LAST Final with commentary by ITV's Brian Moore.**

WENGER WAS ALSO:
The FIRST foreign manager to win the Double

━•◆•◆•◆•━

THE FIRST
PLAYER SENT OFF
IN TWO WORLD CUPS
RIGOBERT SONG, CAMEROON V BRAZIL AT STANFORD STADIUM, ARBORETUM ROAD & GALVEZ STREET, STANFORD, CALIFORNIA, UNITED STATES OF AMERICA, FRIDAY 24 JUNE 1994; CAMEROON V CHILE AT STADE ATLANTIQUE, NANTES, FRANCE, TUESDAY 23 JUNE 1998

There was controversy even before the 1994 match kicked off. The Cameroonians threatened to go on strike unless they were paid promised bonuses from their qualifying matches. They never really stood a chance against the Brazilians who ran out 3-0 winners. In the 84th minute Rigobert Song became, at 17 years and 358 days, the youngest player sent off in a World Cup Finals match. The Cameroonians lost their last match 6-1 to Russia and caught an early plane home. Age seemed not to mature Song and in a petulant game against Chile he was sent off almost four years to the day after elbowing Salas in the 51st minute. His teammate Lauren joined him 47 minutes later in an early bath after he performed a wildly late tackle on the same player. Despite having only nine players, the Cameroonians managed to hold on for a one-all draw, although they caught their usual early plane home. English fans got a closer look at the dreadlocked defender when Gérard Houllier signed him for Liverpool on 26 January 1999 from Seria A side Salernitana for £2.6 million. He never settled at Anfield and made just 38 appearances before he was offloaded to West Ham for £2.5 million in November 2000.

THE FIRST
CHAIRMAN-MANAGER
OF A FOOTBALL LEAGUE TEAM
RON NOADES, BRENTFORD, WEDNESDAY 1 JULY 1998

The former chairman at Crystal Palace, Ron Noades became chairman-manager of Brentford on 1 July 1998 and took the club from Division Three to Division Two. He relinquished control on 20 November 2000.

THE LAST
EUROPEAN CUP WINNERS' CUP FINAL
LAZIO V REAL MALLORCA AT VILLA PARK, TRINITY ROAD, BIRMINGHAM, ENGLAND, WEDNESDAY 19 MAY 1999

The 39th and last winners of the European Cup Winners' Cup were Sven-Göran Eriksson's Lazio, who beat Real Mallorca 2-1. Lazio's goals came from Christian Vieri after seven minutes (he also got a yellow card in the match) and Pavel Nedvěd on 81 minutes. Mallorca scored after 11 minutes through Dani. Uefa decided to revamp the European Cup and Uefa Cup and abolished the Cup Winners' Cup.

THE FIRST
£20 MILLION TRANSFER
INVOLVING AN ENGLISH TEAM
ARSENAL, 1999

Nicolas Anelka signed for Arsenal in February 1997 and quickly made an impression both with other players and the fans. Unfortunately, it was not always a good impression. He earned the nickname 'The Incredible Sulk' after he scored a first half hat-trick against Leicester City on 20 February

1999 but looked miserable for the entire second half. At the end of the season Anelka was named as the Professional Footballers' Association Young Player of the Year (given to a player under 23). Not long after he was on his way out of Highbury and to Real Madrid for £23.5 million. Anelka didn't settle at Madrid either and was soon on the move again. It was not just football teams that Anelka found difficult to get on with. His ex-girlfriend Beth Moutrey recalled:

'We used to have romantic nights in watching films – with his agent. We only ever went out to Tesco. It was embarrassing – I'd get dressed up for a lovely night out and end up at the seafood counter.'

⸻•◦•⸻

THE ONLY
PLAYER TO WIN FULL AND SEMI-PROFESSIONAL ENGLAND CAPS

Steve Guppy, England v Belgium at the Stadium of Light, Sunderland, Tyne & Wear, England, 3 pm Sunday 10 October 1999

Ten years after he was selected for England's semi-professional side while he was playing with then non-league Wycombe Wanderers, Guppy received his only full cap. Kevin Keegan picked Guppy and Frank Lampard to make their debuts in a 2-1 win in a friendly against Belgium.

⸻•◦•⸻

THE FIRST
BRITISH SIDE TO FIELD AN ENTIRELY FOREIGN STARTING LINE-UP

CHELSEA V SOUTHAMPTON AT THE DELL, MILTON ROAD, SOUTHAMPTON, HAMPSHIRE, ENGLAND, BOXING DAY SUNDAY 26 DECEMBER 1999

Chelsea manager Luca Vialli (Italy) chose the following starting line-up: Ed de Goey (Holland), Dan Petrescu (Romania), Emerson Thome (Brazil), Frank Leboeuf (France), Celestine Babayaro (Nigeria), Albert

LAST BRITS STANDING

The match played between Arsenal and Manchester City at the Emirates on 26 August 2007 contained just two British players in the starting line-ups. They were Micah Richards and Michael Johnson, both English and both playing for Manchester City.

Ferrer (Spain), Didier Deschamps (France), Gus Poyet (Uruguay), Roberto di Matteo (Italy), Gabriele Ambrosetti (Italy) and Tore André Flo (Norway). Chelsea won 2-1.

THE LAST
INTERNATIONAL
AT THE OLD WEMBLEY STADIUM
ENGLAND V GERMANY AT WEMBLEY STADIUM, MIDDLESEX, ENGLAND, SATURDAY 7 OCTOBER 2000

The last international played at Wembley saw England pitted against old rivals Germany. Liverpool midfielder Dietmar Hamann scored the only goal of the game with a low free kick from 30 yards as the Germans ran out 1-0 winners. The match – England's 223rd game at Wembley – also marked the last game of Kevin Keegan as England manager and he resigned during the post-match press conference:

'I just feel I fall a little short of what is required in this job. I sat there in the first half and could see things weren't going right, but I couldn't find it in myself to solve the problem.'

It was also **the LAST** match in an England shirt for Arsenal's **Tony Adams.** Adams, **the FIRST England player born after the 1966 World Cup win,** was the last England player to score at Wembley when he hit England's second in a 2-0 win against Ukraine on 31 May 2000.

OTHER LASTS IN THIS MATCH:
The LAST goal scored at the old Wembley Stadium • The LAST match for Kevin Keegan as England manager

THE ONLY

MAN TO MANAGE ENGLAND TWICE

Howard Wilkinson, 1999, 2000

The only man to manage England twice is also the man who never officially became England boss and the last Englishman to manage a team that won the League Championship. When Glenn Hoddle was forced to resign after some unfortunate remarks in 1999, Howard Wilkinson, who had been FA Technical Director since January 1997, took the reins until the appointment of Kevin Keegan. When Keegan decided that he was not up to the job, the FA again turned to Wilkinson to look after the team until Peter Taylor took over, also as caretaker manager, and stayed in situ until England appointed **the First foreign-born manager, Sven-Göran Eriksson**, on 12 January 2001. Wilkinson was in charge for two matches. On 1 February 1999 he picked the team for a friendly against France, which England lost 2-0, and on 11 October 2000 he was in charge when England drew 0-0 in a World Cup qualifying match. (See 1991–1992, page 187.)

THE LAST

SURVIVOR OF THE 1915 FIRST WORLD WAR
FOOTBALL MATCH TRUCE

ALBERT FELSTEAD, PODSMEAD COURT, 155 PODSMEAD ROAD, GLOUCESTER, GLOUCESTERSHIRE, ENGLAND, SUNDAY 22 JULY 2001

In August 1914, two months after the assassination of Archduke Franz Ferdinand, the First World War began. Far from being 'over by Christmas', the bloody conflict raged for more than four years and millions died. On Christmas Day 1915 in the trenches near Laventie, northern France the Germans and the British called a temporary halt to hostilities and the two groups played an impromptu game of football. Bertie Felstead, then 21 and serving with the Royal Welch Fusiliers, was the last survivor of the match. 'There was a bit football if you could call it that – probably 50 or so a side and nobody kept score,' he recalled. A comrade in his regiment was the poet Robert Graves who commemorated the match in his *Christmas Interlude* (1929). Mr Felstead was discharged from the Army in 1916 after being injured at the Battle of the Somme. He died at the age of 106 at an old people's home in Gloucester. He said, 'I was an average man who experienced an extraordinary event. I took part because I loved football. The Germans were all right.'

THE ONLY

FAMILY TO DATE TO SUPPLY
THREE GENERATIONS OF INTERNATIONALS

FEENEY: JAMES MCBURNEY FEENEY, NORTHERN IRELAND V SCOTLAND AT HAMPDEN PARK, MOUNT FLORIDA, GLASGOW, LANARKSHIRE, SCOTLAND, WEDNESDAY 27 NOVEMBER 1946 (DEBUT); WARREN FEENEY, NORTHERN IRELAND V ISRAEL AT TEL AVIV, ISRAEL, WEDNESDAY 3 MARCH 1976 (DEBUT); WARREN FEENEY, NORTHERN IRELAND V LIECHTENSTEIN AT RHEINSPORTPARK, VADUZ LIECHTENSTEIN, WEDNESDAY 27 MARCH 2002 (DEBUT)

While there have been many families supplying footballing brothers and fathers and sons, to date the Feeney family is the only one to supply three generations of internationals. Grandfather Jim (1921–1985), a defender, played for Linfield, Swansea City and Ipswich Town more than 200 times and made two appearances for Northern Ireland. Father Warren (born 1949), a left winger, played for Ards, Linfield, Glentoran and appeared in one match for his country. Son Warren (born 1981), a forward, currently plays for Cardiff City and made his international debut in 2002.

THE LAST

MATCH AT FILBERT STREET

LEICESTER CITY V TOTTENHAM HOTSPUR AT CITY STADIUM, FILBERT STREET, LEICESTER, LEICESTERSHIRE, ENGLAND, 3 PM SATURDAY 11 MAY 2002

City Stadium, more commonly simply known as Filbert Street, was home to Leicester City from 1891 until 2002, its closure being forced by the recommendations of the Taylor Report. The new ground, the Walkers Stadium, opened in August 2002. The last match at Filbert Street was a 2-1 victory over Tottenham Hotspur. Before 21,716 spectators Leicester won 2-1, with goals from Paul Dickov and Matt Piper (the last at the stadium). A penalty from Teddy Sheringham was Spurs' solitary effort. Filbert Street was knocked down in 2003.

THE ONLY
TEAM TO WIN DOUBLE IN THREE SEPARATE DECADES
ARSENAL, 1971, 1998, 2002

Arsenal became the second London side to win the Double when they beat Liverpool 2-1 in the FA Cup Final on 8 May 1971. Manager Bertie Mee was later criticized for dismantling the side too quickly as the team fell into a slump in the mid-1970s. Terry Neill began the resurgence, leading the side to three consecutive FA Cup Finals and a European final, but only winning one. When he was sacked George Graham took the helm and the glory days seemed to return to Arsenal Stadium, only for his reign to end in disgrace over the bungs scandal. Arsène Wenger became the first foreign manager of the Gunners and won the Double for the club in his first full season in charge, repeating the feat four years later.

THE ONLY
MAN TO WIN THE DOUBLE AS A PLAYER AND A MEMBER OF THE COACHING STAFF
PAT RICE, ARSENAL, 1971, 1998, 2002

Right back Pat Rice holds the unique position of being the only man to have won the Double as a player (1971) and as a member of the coaching staff (1998, 2002) of the same club. In 1980 he also became **the FIRST player to appear in five FA Cup Finals for the same club.**

THE ONLY
WORLD CUP
HOSTED IN TWO COUNTRIES
JAPAN AND SOUTH KOREA, 2002

The World Cup has traditionally been held in one country, but for the first time in 2002 Fifa split the hosting duties between two countries. The competition was held between 31 May and 30 June 2002, with the final between Germany and Brazil being held at Yokohama, Japan. On 12 June Claudio Caniggia added to the reputation of his countrymen for being dismissed when he became **the FIRST player sent off in a World Cup while sitting on the substitute's bench** in Argentina's match against Sweden, which ended in a one-all draw.

THIS MATCH WAS ALSO:
The FIRST and, to date, ONLY World Cup held in Asia

THE LAST
MATCH AT MAINE ROAD
Manchester City v Southampton at Maine Road, Moss Side, Manchester, England, Sunday 11 May 2003

Maine Road opened on 23 August 1923 and at the time was the largest club ground in England and the second largest in the country after Wembley Stadium. Eleven years later 84,569 people crowded into Maine Road to watch an FA Cup tie between Manchester City and Stoke City, a record for an English club ground. With the Taylor Report

---

TO THE DOG HOUSE
Maine Road was originally called Dog Kennel Lane and was part of an old road to the south of Manchester.

recommending all-seater stadia, Maine Road's capacity was reduced to 35,150. The club looked for a new home and at the start of the 2003–2004 season moved to the newly built City of Manchester Stadium in east Manchester. Maine Road was demolished in 2004. The last game at the stadium saw City lose 1-0 to Southampton, with Michael Svensson scoring the final goal. Marc-Vivien Foe hit **the LAST goal scored by a City player at the ground** on 26 April 2003. Tragically, he died exactly two months later while playing for Cameroon.

•◆•

THE FIRST
INDOORS FA CUP FINAL
Arsenal v Southampton at Millennium Stadium, Westgate Street, Cardiff, Glamorgan, Wales, Saturday 17 May 2003

In a repeat of 1978–1980, Arsenal returned to three consecutive FA Cup Finals. In the third they faced Southampton. There were 73,726 spectators at the match and due to poor weather the game was played indoors, as the roof was closed. David Seaman, in his last appearance for the club, donned the captain's armband. Arsenal wore their usual red and white strip, but as with the game against Liverpool two years earlier, their opponents wore what had been Arsenal's normal away strip of yellow and blue. The game has quickly been forgotten, but Robert Pirès scored the winning goal for the Gunners in the 38th minute.

•◆•

THE ONLY
ENGLAND MANAGER KNOWN TO HAVE HAD AN AFFAIR WITH AN FA SECRETARY
SVEN-GÖRAN ERIKSSON, JUNE 2004

An unlikely looking Lothario, Sven-Göran Eriksson, **the First foreigner to manage England**, arrived in the country in January 2001 with his

Italian lawyer girlfriend Nancy Dell'Olio. In August 2004 it was revealed that he had been having an affair with Faria Alam, a beautiful 37-year-old Bangladeshi secretary to Football Association executive director David Davies, who simultaneously had been sharing her favours with FA chief executive Mark Palios, 51, who resigned when the story broke. An industrial tribunal rejected Alam's claims against the FA of sexual harassment, unfair dismissal and breach of contract. Alam gave interviews to *The Mail on Sunday* and the *News of the World* detailing the affairs and appeared on *Celebrity Big Brother* in January 2006 where on 17 January she was the second celebrity voted off (after Jodie Marsh).

IN FEBRUARY 2007 THE **NEWS OF THE WORLD** RAN A STORY THAT CLAIMED, '**FA sex scandal secretary Faria Alam is a secret £8,000-a-night hooker**'.

THE ONLY
PROFESSIONAL FOOTBALLER TO ADVERTISE VIAGRA
PELÉ, JANUARY 2005

The world's greatest footballer began advertising the impotence treatment in early 2005, although he made it clear that he had never actually suffered from the affliction. Pfizer, the drug's manufacturer, hired Pelé to get the message across in Europe, Asia and South America with a campaign of print and television advertising. In Brazil the government banned the TV campaign after it became alarmed by a sharp increase in illicit use of anti-impotence drugs by young people. (See 1971, page 147).

THE FIRST
FA CUP FINAL DECIDED ON PENALTIES
ARSENAL V MANCHESTER UNITED AT MILLENNIUM STADIUM, WESTGATE STREET, CARDIFF, GLAMORGAN, WALES, SATURDAY 21 MAY 2005

On what was becoming an annual trip to Cardiff for either Arsenal or bitter enemies Manchester United, the teams lined up in front of 71,876 fans. There followed 120 goalless minutes – the first final without goals since 1912. Then the FA Cup was decided on penalties for the first time. José Antonio Reyes was sent off in the last minute of extra time for fouling Cristiano Ronaldo. When it came to the penalties Jens Lehmann made a brilliant save to defy Paul Scholes and Patrick Vieira put the ball past United's Roy Carroll to win the game 5-4 for Arsenal. It was Vieira's last kick for the Gunners before leaving Highbury for a new life in Italy with Juventus.

THE FIRST
ENGLAND CAPTAIN SENT OFF
DAVID BECKHAM, ENGLAND V AUSTRIA AT OLD TRAFFORD, MANCHESTER, ENGLAND, SATURDAY 8 OCTOBER 2005

On 30 June 1998 David Beckham had petulantly kicked out after being fouled by Diego Simeone in England's match against Argentina at St Etienne in the World Cup. For his effort Beckham was sent off and the match ended in a 2-2 draw, thanks to goals from Alan Shearer and Michael Owen. England lost the penalty shoot-out, causing many fans to blame the squeaky-voiced Beckham. The clotheshorse player was then burned in effigy in England. Seven years later, Beckham forgiven and appointed international captain, was dismissed again to become the first England player wearing the captain's armband to be so shamed when he received a red card in a World Cup qualifier against Austria which, despite his behaviour, England won 1-0.

DAVID BECKHAM IS ALSO:
The ONLY England player sent off twice

THE FIRST
ENGLISH TEAM TO BEAT
REAL MADRID AT THE BERNABÉU
REAL MADRID V ARSENAL AT SANTIAGO BERNABÉU, MADRID, SPAIN, TUESDAY 21 FEBRUARY 2006

With few giving them a chance, Arsenal travelled to Real Madrid for the First Leg of the Second Round Champions League match. However, the

Gunners overwhelmed the Spaniards and took the lead through a 47th minute goal from Thierry Henry. David Beckham missed two chances, including a sitter that Arsenal keeper Jens Lehmann easily saved. Arsenal drew the Second Leg 0-0 at Highbury on 8 March 2006 to go through.

THE LAST
MATCH AT ARSENAL STADIUM

Arsenal v Wigan Athletic at Arsenal Stadium, Avenell Road, Highbury, London, England, Sunday 7 May 2006

The FIRST game played at Arsenal Stadium was a Division Two match on Saturday 6 September 1913 against Leicester Fosse. Tommy Benfield of Leicester scored the first goal at the new ground and George Jobey scored the first Arsenal goal as the Gunners ran out 2-1 winners. The last game played there was on 7 May 2006 against Wigan Athletic. Arsenal won 4-2 with a hat-trick from Thierry Henry. That summer the bulldozers moved in to turn the stadium into Highbury Square, a series of 711 small and costly apartments with the pitch area becoming a communal garden. The East and West Stands have been preserved in the new development, opened in 2010. The development topped out on 6 March 2008.

THIS MATCH ALSO WITNESSED:
The LAST hat-trick scored at Arsenal Stadium

THE ONLY
WORLD CUP PLAYER SHOWN A YELLOW CARD
THREE TIMES IN THE SAME MATCH
JOSIP ŠIMUNIĆ, CROATIA V AUSTRALIA AT GOTTLIEB-DAIMLER STADIUM, STUTTGART, GERMANY, 9 PM THURSDAY 22 JUNE 2006

The final match in Group F of the World Cup saw Croatia with one point facing Australia with three to see who would qualify for the next round of the competition. The Aussies had comprehensively beaten Japan 3-1 in their opening match and the single Croatian point had come from their goalless draw also against Japan, so although the Aussies were favourites, either team could have qualified. The referee and linesmen all came from England – Graham Poll, Philip Sharp and Glen Turner respectively. After just two minutes Croatia took the lead through winger Darijo Srna. The match was tightly and fiercely fought. On 32 minutes Dario Šimić's name became the first to go into Poll's book. Six minutes later a foul by Igor Tudor resulted in Poll awarding the Aussies a penalty and Tudor being the second Croatian shown a yellow card. Defender Craig Moore hit the back of the net to equalize the scores and that was the way the score stayed at half-time.

Eleven minutes after the restart Croatia's captain Niko Kovač put his country into the lead for the second time. In the 61st minute Graham Poll showed Josip Šimunić the yellow card and eight minutes after that Croatia's goalkeeper Stipe Pletikosa followed Šimunić into the referee's notebook. The last 15 minutes of the match were the most controversial. On 79 minutes Harry Kewell, married to former Emmerdale star Sheree Murphy, pulled the score back to two-all. A minute later Brett Emerton became the first Australian booked and five minutes later Poll showed the red card to Dario Šimić. Then in the 87th minute Brett Emerton was sent off. Three minutes later Josip Šimunić received his second yellow card of the match, but Poll, seemingly unaware that he had already booked the Croatian, didn't produce a red card. Neither of the linesmen noticed the discrepancy either. Then with three minutes of added time gone Poll booked Šimunić for a third time and finally showed him the red card to make him the third player sent off in the match but the only one in World Cup history shown a yellow card three times in the same match.

Until his blunder Poll, the only English referee at the tournament, had been a possibility to take charge of the Final, but on 28 June he was sacked by Fifa from taking charge of any of the remaining games. The next day Poll announced his retirement from international refereeing at the end of the World Cup:

'What I did was an error in law. There can be no dispute. It was not caused by a Fifa directive, it was not caused by me being asked to referee differently to the way I referee in the Premier League. The laws of the game are very specific.

The referee takes responsibility for his actions on the field of play. I was the referee that evening. It was my error and the buck stops with me.'

THE LAST
MATCH AT BELLE VUE

Doncaster Rovers v Nottingham Forest at Belle Vue Ground, Doncaster, South Yorkshire, England, Saturday 23 December 2006

Having survived the ignominy of having the club chairman trying to burn it down, Belle Vue survived as the home of Doncaster Rovers until 2006 when the club relocated to the Keepmoat Stadium. The first game had been on 26 August 1922 against Gainsborough Trinity. The last was against Nottingham Forest, at the time League One leaders. Rovers won 1-0 with the last goal at the stadium being scored by Theo Streete. At 3.17 am on 7 February 2007 a large gas explosion wrecked more than half of the Main Stand and injured two people nearby. (See 1995, page 200.)

THE FIRST
PROFESSIONAL MATCH AT THE NEW WEMBLEY STADIUM

ENGLAND U-21 V ITALY U-21 AT WEMBLEY STADIUM, MIDDLESEX, ENGLAND, SATURDAY 24 MARCH 2007

After what seemed like interminable delays caused by litigation and financial matters and at a cost of £798 million, the new Wembley Stadium was handed over to the Football Association on 9 March 2007, four years behind schedule. Still controversial, the pitch, which is 13 ft (4 m) lower than the previous one, has been criticized by several managers including

Arsène Wenger, Sir Alex Ferguson and David Moyes, and has been re-laid five times since 2007. **The FIRST football match at the stadium** was between building workers and Wembley staff. A charity match was the first before spectators. The first match featuring professionals was between the U-21 teams from England and Italy before 55,700 fans. The first player to score was Italian striker Giampaolo Pazzini after 28 seconds – he went on to get a hat-trick as the game finished 3-3. **The FIRST Englishman to get his name on the score sheet** was David Bentley.

THIS MATCH ALSO SAW:
The FIRST goal scored at the new Wembley Stadium

━━•◄►•━━

THE FIRST
FOOTBALL MATCH
PLAYED AT CROKE PARK
IRELAND V WALES AT CROKE PARK, JONES ROAD, DUBLIN, IRELAND, SATURDAY 24 MARCH 2007

The location that is now Croke Park has been the spiritual home of Gaelic football since 1884 and many purists believe that it is wrong to allow other sports to play there. The renovated Croke Park (Páirc an Chrócaigh) opened in 1913. It is the largest sports stadium in Ireland and the principal stadium and headquarters of the Gaelic Athletic Association, Ireland's biggest sporting organization. Seven years later, on 21 November 1920, the IRA murdered 14 British officers in their beds in a concerted operation mainly in south inner city Dublin. Later that day at 3.25 pm the Black and Tans had their revenge, opening fire on the 8,000-strong crowd at a Gaelic football match between Dublin and Tipperary at Croke Park. (The Black and Tans were the Royal Irish Constabulary Reserve Force, one of two paramilitary forces emplyed from 1920–1921 to suppress revolution in Ireland by targeting the IRA. The nickname came about because they wore khaki trousers and navy British police uniforms, and also refers to the nickname of a famous pack of foxhounds from Limerick.) Seven people died immediately including one of the players, Michael Hogan, and five were fatally wounded.

The first rugby match was played there on 11 February 2007 between Ireland and France. On 24 February Ireland played England in a match that could have been inflammatory because of the events in 1920, but passed off peacefully. The first football match at Croke Park was played between Ireland and Wales in a qualifying match for Euro '2008 and Ireland won by a single goal scored, appropriately enough, by Stephen Ireland.

━•◆•━

THE FIRST

FA CUP FINAL
AT THE NEW WEMBLEY STADIUM

CHELSEA V MANCHESTER UNITED AT WEMBLEY STADIUM,
MIDDLESEX, ENGLAND, SATURDAY 19 MAY 2007

Roman Abramovich's Blues met the Red Devils of Manchester in the first FA Cup Final at Wembley after the competition had relocated from its temporary home at the Millennium Stadium in Cardiff. Just one goal – from Chelsea's Didier Drogba – separated the teams.

DIDIER DROGBA WAS: The FIRST player to score in an
FA Cup Final at the new Wembley Stadium

LAST IN, FIRST OUT

Chelsea were the last winners of the FA Cup at the old Wembley and the first winners at the new.

THE FIRST

3D LIVE SPORTING EVENT

ARSENAL V MANCHESTER UNITED AT EMIRATES STADIUM, ASHBURTON GROVE, LONDON, ENGLAND, SUNDAY 31 JANUARY 2010

On the last Sunday in January 2010 Sky Sports broadcast the world's first live 3D sporting event – the Premiership clash between Arsenal and Manchester United. Fans wearing special spectacles in nine pubs in London, Manchester, Cardiff, Edinburgh and Dublin watched the match. Filming the action at a variety of angles were 16 high-definition cameras at Arsenal's Emirates Stadium and it was shown on Sky 3D, Europe's first dedicated 3D channel. United won 3-1 thanks to a goal each from Wayne Rooney and Ji-Sung Park and an opening goal by Arsenal's gaffe-prone goalkeeper Manuel Almunia. Centre back Thomas Vermaelen scored a consolation for the Gunners ten minutes from time. So the world's first football goal to be shown in 3D was an own goal.

THE FIRST

PLAYER JAILED
FOR A VIOLENT TACKLE

MARK CHAPMAN, WARWICK CROWN COURT, NORTHGATE SOUTH SIDE, WARWICK, WARWICKSHIRE, THURSDAY 4 MARCH 2010

Playing for Long Lawford against Wheeltappers in a Rugby and District Sunday League match in Warwickshire in October 2009, and with his side 3-1 down and the referee about to blow the final whistle, Mark Chapman, 20, went in for a reckless sliding tackle on 26-year-old left back Terry Johnson, shattering his leg in two places. The referee showed Chapman the red card and then the player found himself being prosecuted for the tackle. Sentencing him to six months in prison, Judge Robert Orme declared, 'This is a deliberate act, a premeditated act. A football match gives no one any excuse to carry out wanton violence.' An FA spokesman commented:

'It's the first time anyone has been sent to prison for a tackle. There have been two cases where people were sent to prison for other incidents on the pitch, but nothing like this.'

BIBLIOGRAPHY

BOOKS

Ball, Alan, *Ball of Fire*, Pelham Books, London, 1967

Barrett, Norman, *The Daily Telegraph Football Chronicle*, (7th ed.), Carlton Books, London, 2004

Batty, Clive, *The England Compendium*, Vision Sports Publishing, London, 2005

Batty, Clive, *The Vision Book of Football Records 2010*, Vision Sports Publishing, London, 2009

Beadle, Jeremy, *Jeremy Beadle's Today's the Day*, W.H. Allen, London, 1979

Best, George with Ross Benson, *The Good, the Bad and the Bubbly*, Pan, London, 1990

Best, George and Graeme Wright, *Where Do I Go From Here? An Autobiography*, Futura, London, 1982

Bolam, Mike, *The Newcastle Miscellany*, Vision Sports Publishing, London, 2007

Butler, David and Gareth Butler, *Twentieth-Century British Political Facts, 1900–2000*, Macmillan, London, 2000

Collett, Mike, *The Guinness Record of the FA Cup*, Guinness, London, 1993

Collins, Mick, *Roy of the Rovers: The Unauthorised Biography*, Aurum, London, 2008

Donnelley, Paul, *The Arsenal Companion*, Pitch Publishing, Brighton, 2008

Donnelley, Paul, *Arsenal: On This Day*, Pitch Publishing, Brighton, 2009

Freddi, Cris, *Complete Book of the World Cup 2006*, HarperSport, London, 2006

Hayes, Dean, *Arsenal: The Football Facts*, John Blake, London, 2007

Hugman, Barry J., *Rothmans Football League Players' Records: The Complete A-Z 1946–1981*, Rothmans Publications, Aylesbury, 1981

Kutner, Jon and Spencer Leigh, *1000 UK Number One Hits*, Omnibus, London, 2005

Maidment, Jem, *The Official Arsenal 100 Greatest Games*, Hamlyn, London, 2005

Matthew, H.C.G. and Sir Brian Harrison (eds.) *Oxford Dictionary of National Biography*, Oxford University Press, Oxford, 2004

McElroy, Robert, *The Rangers Miscellany*, Vision Sports Publishing, London, 2008

McWhirter, Norris (ed.), *The Guinness Book of Records 1984*, London, Guinness, 1983

Morrison, Ian, *The World Cup: A Complete Record 1930–1990*, Breedon Books, Derby, 1990

Motson, John, *Motson's FA Cup Odyssey: The World's Greatest Knockout Competition*, Robson Books, London, 2005

Motson, John, *Motson's World Cup Extravaganza: Football's Greatest Drama 1930–2006*, Robson Books, London, 2006

Moynihan, Leo, *The Liverpool Miscellany*, Vision Sports Publishing, London, 2007

Murray, Scott and Rowan Walker, *Day of the Match*, Boxtree, London, 2008

Nicholson, Vivian and Stephen Smith, *Spend, Spend, Spend*, Fontana, London, 1978

O'Brien, Mark, *The Everton Miscellany*, Vision Sports Publishing, London, 2008

Oliver, Guy, *The Guinness Book of World Soccer*, (2nd ed.), Guinness, London, 1995

Ollier, Fred, *Arsenal: A Complete Record 1886–1988*, Breedon Books, Derby, 1988

Peskett, Roy (ed.), *Tom Whittaker's Arsenal Story*, Sporting Handbook, London, 1958

Ponting, Ivan, *The Book of Football Obituaries*, Know The Score, Studley, 2008

Ponting, Ivan, *Manchester United Player by Player*, (8th ed.), Know The Score, Studley, 2008

Ponting, Ivan, *Liverpool Player by Player*, (6th ed.), Know The Score, Studley, 2009

Powley, Adam and Martin Cloake, *The Spurs Miscellany*, Vision Sports Publishing, London, 2006

Robertson, Patrick, *The New Shell Book of Firsts*, Headline, London, 1994

Robinson, John, *Soccer Firsts*, Guinness, London, 1986

Rollin, Jack (ed.), *The Guinness Book of Soccer Facts and Feats*, (3rd ed.), Guinness, London, 1980

Rollin, Jack and Glenda Rollin (current eds.) *Rothmans Football Yearbook* (various editions)

Scott, Les, *End to End Stuff: The Essential Football Book*, Bantam Press, London, 2008

Seddon, Peter, *The World Cup's Strangest Moments*, Robson Books, London, 2005

Seddon, Peter, *Pickles the World Cup Dog and Other Unusual Football Obituaries*, Aurum, London, 2007

Smith, Andrew *The Celtic Miscellany*, Vision Sports Publishing, London, 2008

White, John *The Celtic Football Miscellany*, Carlton Books, London, 2006

White, John, *The England Football Miscellany*, Carlton Books, London, 2006

White, John, *The Liverpool Football Miscellany*, Carlton Books, London, 2006

White, John, *The Rangers Football Miscellany*, Carlton Books, London, 2006

Williams, Tony (ed.) *Football League Club Directory* (various editions)

Wilson, Bob, *Life in the Beautiful Game*, Icon Books, Thriplow, 2008

Woodhall, Dave, *The Aston Villa Miscellany*, Vision Sports Publishing, London, 2008

NEWSPAPERS

The Daily Telegraph; The Guardian; The Herald; The Independent;
The Observer; The Times; The Times of India

WEBSITES

www.astonvillaplayerdatabase.com
www.ayresomepark.co.uk
bbc.co.uk
www.black-history-month.co.uk
www.thebusbybabes.com
community.footballpools.com
www.cricketarchive.com
www.cwgc.org
www.earthtimes.org
www.11v11.co.uk
en.wikipedia.org
www.england-afc.co.uk
www.englandfootballonline.com
www.englandstats.com
www.evertonresults.com
www.fa-cupfinals.co.uk
www.footballgroundguide.com
www.guardian.co.uk
www.imdb.com
www.kerrydalestreet.com
www.la84foundation.org
www.leicestercity-mad.co.uk
www.lfchistory.net

www.liverpoolfc.tv
www.liverweb.org.uk
www.mightyleeds.co.uk
national.soccerhall.org
nifootball.blogspot.com
www.planetworldcup.com
www.rangers.premiumtv.co.uk
www.redandwhitekop.com
www.rsssf.com
www.scottishfa.co.uk
scottish-football-historical-archive.com
www.soccerbase.com
www.the-staffordshire-encyclopaedia.co.uk
www.thestatcat.co.uk
www.stretfordend.co.uk
www.theborofc.info
www.thewolvessite.co.uk
www.timesonline.co.uk
weekendwonders.co.uk
www.wereldvanoranje.nl
www.yeoviltownyears.com
www.youtube.com